DISABLE YOUR LABELS

How Overcoming Toxic Situations, Can Empower our Youth, and Change Their Future

DESIRAE KING

Ordering Information

Quantity sales: Special discounts are available on quantity purchases by corporations, associations, and others. For details, contact the publisher at the address above.

Orders by U.S. trade bookstores and wholesalers:

Please contact Desirae King
Email: DisableYourLabels@gmail.com

Printed in the United States of America
ISBN-13: 978-1691114337

ACKNOWLEDGEMENTS

The summers used to feel as cold as winters when you first passed away. If it was up to me, you would still be here, alive, and well. The fact remains that you are gone, but your love still flows in my heart, mind, and spirit. I can't thank you enough for all of the sacrifices that you made and the time and love that you gave. You paved the way for me and the generations after me. I just hope that I can pass some of the same knowledge, morals, and principles down to the next generation the way that you did for me.

I dedicate this book to my great aunt Shirley, aka "Buttercup". It has been said that before she passed, she was waiting for me to come see her at the hospital. The day that I arrived, I watched her go through the rehabilitation process, learned to speak her first words all over again, and then, unbelievably, the very next day I received the news that she had taken her last breath. In life, we all have regrets. We have those things that we wish that we could have done differently. My biggest regret, to this day, was not living up to my full potential while you were still alive, Aunt Shirley. It took your passing away for me to start to really walk in my greatness and stop being hindered by my fears.

I would like to also thank my grandmother, Dorothy Sanders, aka Mrs. Sanders (or "Dot"), and also my grandfathers: Donald King, Curtis Sanders, aka "SugarRay", and FaFa.

To my father, Aunt Ann, Aunt Shay, and Aunt Desiree (whom I was named after), your deaths will never be in vain. You will always live through me.

To Granny, Net, and Chris, it hurts me the most when the three of you passed away. There were so many wonderful things I wanted us to do together. You all always believed in me.

Toot, we still see your smile at every spades game, at every family gathering, and in everything we do. We lost a good one when we lost you. The pain in our hearts will eventually subside, but it doesn't change the fact that we miss you so much. You know that on every birthday I'm going to still rep #TeamPiscesForever!

To Shawn, my children's Godfather, the blessing that you have been to our family will remain priceless. When I didn't believe in myself, you believed in me. When I felt down, you were always the hand that lifted me up. You could always tell when I was going through something, and the Holy Spirit would lead you straight to me. You would know just how to give me the encouragement that I needed.

I love each one of you, and thank you for impacting my life in such a major way. I dedicate this book to those that are gone but never forgotten, and also the families affected by the 2017 Las Vegas Shooting Massacre. #VEGASSTRONG

TABLE OF CONTENTS

CHAPTER ONE

Abandoned at an Early Age

"At some point, you have to realize that there are certain people who can stay in your heart but not in your life."

- *Anonymous*

"Where's my mommy?"

I tried to quiet my little brother, but I was only two years older than him at the tender age of five, so it only resulted in me clumsily trying to cover his mouth and him getting more upset. We were sitting on the brown couch in the living room. For some strange reason, the brown of the couch stands out with laser clarity in my mind. Not a walnut color or a pecan brown. Not a light caramel brown or chestnut. No! it was the color of an aging oak tree's bark, right before the beginning of a long winter, as the leaves were just starting to wilt and forgetting how alive they were just months before. We sat there, not knowing that our own long winter was coming. We were waiting for our mother to return home. She never did.

Even at such a young age, my maternal instinct kicked in. I was used to watching out for my younger brother. Just about a year earlier, I had stood bravely between him and my mother's previous boyfriend. To the rest of the world, this man looked like your average, run of the mill twenty-nine-year-old, but to me, he was a gigantic monster. He was big and tall, with the largest hands I had ever seen. I watched in horror as he tried to use those hands to touch my brother, who was only two and a half at the time. The Giant was trying to crawl into bed with him. I took a deep breath, put my hands at my hips, and mustered up all of the courage I possibly could.

#DisableYourLabels

"STOP!" I yelled, as loud as I could, standing in the doorway of the bedroom.

His head whipped around to face me, eyes opened wide.

"STOP! Don't touch him. Don't you touch my baby brother!"

The Giant listened to me, and he left my brother alone. Unfortunately, my defiance only led to him turning that attention onto me. He began touching me inappropriately whenever my mother wasn't around instead. To say that I was relieved when he and my mother split up would be an understatement.

Now, here we were, all alone. I told myself to be strong for my brother once again. Sure, we were both afraid. My mind would often wander towards thinking that she might be dead. Most of all, I wanted to just protect my brother and make sure that he was alright. We fell asleep on that awful brown couch together, and when we woke up, realizing that she still wasn't home, the real anxiety began to kick in. I didn't know what that feeling was at the time, but I recognized the fear, the uneasiness, and the overwhelming sadness.

Why is she not coming home? What did I do wrong? I knew it. I knew I wasn't good enough. Will I ever see mommy again?

Was it me? I wondered. What could I have possibly done better to have changed her mind? How could I have made her stay?

We asked her boyfriend where she was several times. He didn't know what to tell us. Gus was an older gentleman, probably about twenty years my mother's senior. He tried to be very careful about what he said in response to our questions, not revealing any of the grown-up secrets that children weren't supposed to hear. Even though he meant well and was only trying to protect us from the truth of the situation, his discretion resulted in us being totally in the dark about what was happening to us. More than ever, I felt as though I wasn't a good enough daughter. Somehow, I had failed. That was the only explanation that made sense in my racing five-year-old mind.

Gus wasn't like the Giant. I didn't have to worry about him touching either of us or doing anything that would make us feel uncomfortable. My brother and I were relatively safe with him during that scary time, but of course, that didn't help alleviate the distress that we were feeling. No matter how kind he may have tried to be, Gus wasn't Mommy. Although he made sure that our basic needs were met, we felt forgotten, and we were both terrified.

Two or three days later, Gus finally called my grandfather. He solemnly came to pick us up, and I can remember my grandfather dressing the two of us for church. With blank looks on our faces, we wore our Sunday dress, our perfectly pressed clothing covering the chaos that brewed beneath the surface.

We had no idea that this would be the last time my brother and I would live together. There is a picture of us dressed to the tee, totally oblivious that we would be separated that day. My grandfather phoned my brother's grandmother, who came to pick him up. My brother's paternal grandparents raised him for the rest of his childhood. We would only see each other once or twice within the next seven years as we were growing up.

As for me, I remember going from family member to family member over the next two years and overhearing them speaking in hushed tones to one another.

"I don't want her..."

"You know I'm going through my own problems right now, I can't..."

"Ain't no way I can take care of a small child right now..."

During that confusing period of our lives, I also recall finally finding out the real reason why Mommy had disappeared. I didn't fully understand, but as I began to eavesdrop on more of the family adult conversations, I was able to piece together an ambiguous explanation.

"... oh, she ain't dead. She isn't foolin' anybody. She's somewhere getting high!"

"She on them drugs..."

"You know good and well she out there..."

I would later find out that Gus wasn't involved in the drugs that were taking over my mother's life at that time, and he just loved her for who she was, without judgement. He had no idea that she would go as far as abandoning her children. Her disappearance was as big of a shock to him as it was to us.

Eventually, and thankfully, I ended up with my great aunt Shirley, who was my grandfather's sister. She showed me the love and care that I was craving from my absent mother, even though it could never really be the same. When I was about seven or eight years old, I had the most vivid dream about my mother while I was still living with my great aunt. In that dream, she was wearing an old-fashioned black and white striped prison uniform. Not too long after that premonition, my mother actually did go to jail for about six months for a parole violation. She had tested positive for drugs on two previous occasions, and then she produced another dirty urine test a third time, confirming what the family members had said about her habit. Those six months were probably the best thing that could have happened to her at the time to get her off the street. As a matter of fact, here is a letter she wrote to me from in prison over 20 years ago.

Hi Kee Kee!   9-16-94

          It's about 3 or 4
in the morning, and
I just had a bad
dream about you, some
kind of way you were
took from me, and I
was in so much pain,
and I couldn't find
you, and I looked and
looked for you but
you were gone, I
don't know if the
"Devil's" busy playing
tricks on me, or are
you in some kind of
pain, whatever it is
dear, Don't hold it in

we'll be like pen pals (smile) I love you so much, don't ever forget it. I guess God might be telling me to get my act together, or you will be really taken from me for good. Remember one thing within your heart don't give up on me, pray for me, I'm not a bad person I made a mistake I used drugs. But that part of my life is over now, and looking forward to renew ing my relationship with you and Daniel some day soon. (O.K.)

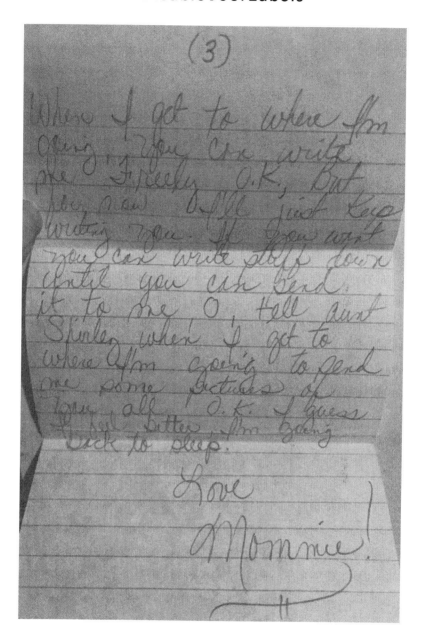

Once my mother was released from prison she was still in and out of my life. In the fourth grade, my mother was in and out of my life, although I didn't live with her. Sometimes, she would promise to show up and she wouldn't. Over and over again I'd get all dressed up, my heart set on being able to finally hang out with my mom. After waiting on the stairs for hours, I would move towards the front of the house. Maybe it would be better if she could see me from the street. Maybe she would show up faster then. *She probably just needs to see me from up the block*, I told myself.

"Girl, get your butt inside this house! It's freezing out there!" Aunt Shirley would yell from inside.

"I'm waiting for Mommy!" She just didn't understand. Twisting my neck in anger, I ignored her commands. Any other time, she would've nipped my disobedience in the bud right then and there, but I believed that she was trying to be patient with me because of the situation.

I would always take my disappointment out on Aunt Shirley. As if it was her fault that my mother didn't care enough to keep her promises to her oldest child, as if it was her fault that I didn't have a mom around to show me how to be a young woman, as if it was her fault that I was stuck being raised by an old lady who didn't understand at all what I was going through during those adolescent years.

Aunt Shirley was trying her very best to provide for me. If she bought something for herself, she would buy a smaller one for me. Having raised three sons of her own, she cared for me like the daughter she never had. Her love was evident, and I didn't want to seem ungrateful. All I wanted was a pair of light-up LA Gear tennis shoes, and here was Aunt Shirley buying me a fur coat just like hers. What nine-year-old child do you know who owns her own fur coat?

I remember some of my fondest memories during those times were of hanging out with my home girl, Tasha, who had a young mom. Her mom had a cool little hip car, and she would take us out and we would all have fun. I inwardly resented not having that same relationship with my mother. That disappointment and resentment morphed into a number of behavioral problems in school.

I will never forget a time when after becoming frustrated with me during one of those difficult times in school, my fourth-grade teacher, Ms. Paris, leaned on close to me and stared me down over the top of her bifocal glasses. The older white woman didn't like me one bit, and the feeling was mutual. She limped closer to me. Her massive stomach and the saggy pale skin of her upper arms shook uncontrollably as she wagged her finger in my face. I tried not to retch at the putrid combination of smells coming from her body. Her breath smelled like stale coffee and fresh cigarettes, and I stared at her yellow teeth in disgust. Small drops of spit escaped her mouth as she spoke.

"Little girl, keep this up, ya hear? Keep up this behavior, and you won't be nothing in life. You're going to end up a dopeman's bitch, pregnant, and on welfare. Is that what you want?!"

My eyes grew wide.

Even though that was an incredibly hurtful thing to have been said to me as a nine-year-old child, it was also one of the only times I could remember my mother coming to my rescue and standing up for me. Once she heard what had happened, most likely from Aunt Shirley, she came up to the school and cussed ugly old Ms. Paris out for speaking to me in that way.

Things continued that way for a few years, and then when I was twelve and in the seventh grade, Aunt Shirley sat me down and let me know that I would be able to go back and live with my mother, who was staying with Gus, again. I didn't know what to think. She wanted to make sure that I would be okay with going back over there again. Since I had become accustomed to trying to not get in anyone's way or be a burden, I agreed before I could even really think about what that meant. I let Aunt Shirley know that it was okay, and I wanted to go and try to live with my mother.

The time that she spent in jail seemed to help my mother kicked her drug habit. I remember that year and a half fondly. Mommy would blast Mary J. Blige loudly on her radio, and we would cook together, sing and laugh in the kitchen. There was always music playing in the house while Mommy cleaned. She loved to watch the Def Comedy Jam series hosted by Martin Lawrence, but she didn't want me to watch those shows because of all of the cursing that would come from the comedian's mouths. I would sneak into her room and watch the VCR tapes when she wasn't around to see what made Mommy laugh so much behind closed doors.

Even though I can recall happy times, finally living with my mother after all of those years of longing for her presence, I also remember the darkness that hung over that time, as well. There was a strange routine that I was forced to follow in my mother and Gus' home. Gus insisted that I needed to take two showers a day, no matter what, in the morning and at night. The shower was in their master bedroom, and there was no door to the bathroom. Now, every time I showered, Gus would always be in their room, and it was such that the mirrors in the bathroom and bedroom would easily allow anyone in the room to see everything that was going on in the shower. I would nervously remove my clothes and attempt to cover my nakedness with towels. At that age, I was a young girl coming into my womanhood, and I had already developed the curvy figure that I still have to this day. He never tried anything with me, but he definitely made sure to be awake and present when I was taking my frequent showers.

One day, I eventually found the courage to discuss my apprehension about this routine with Aunt Shirley. Her eyes narrowed while she listened to me, confirming that what I was feeling was valid. She asked me if my mother was aware of all of this, and when I nodded silently, she sucked her teeth.

"Oh, hell no!" She said angrily under her breath.

Not too long after telling her about that, I was living back with Aunt Shirley. Before she found out about the shower situation, Aunt Shirley had moved into a senior citizens home. Once she had made sure that I was okay with my mother, she had felt comfortable enough to make her move. She wanted to make sure all was okay with me before she did that, because the senior citizens home did not allow children to reside there.

However, when I told her about how I felt about Gus, she insisted that I come back to live with her. I began sneaking in and out of her new place, so that no one else would know that I was living there. She protected me, cared for me, and wouldn't allow me to stay in a situation that she felt may be unsafe for me. I will always thank her for that. I don't know how happy those nosey old folks were at the senior citizens home, though.

They would whisper under their breaths, "Watch! Watch that little girl. It's 7:59AM in the morning. Now what she doin' comin' out that house?" I ignored them and kept moving.

I didn't return back to living with my mother until she began dating the man that I would learn to love as my stepfather, Reggie. I felt extremely safe with Reggie, her new boyfriend. I always wished that Reggie was my real father. Even if my mother would forget to feed me, Reggie always made sure that I ate. I had the utmost respect for that man, and I lived there with them until I graduated high school. My mother had a fresh start along with a steady job. Reggie didn't know about her drug habit, and if she was still using while she was with him, she definitely hid it very well.

Before meeting Reggie, I had never known what it felt like to have a positive male role model in the home. Have you ever had to tell someone that you were allergic to seafood or shellfish? I have to do it all the time. The look on the person's face is almost always the same. They can't believe that you aren't able to enjoy shrimp, lobster, or crab. Sometimes, their eyes grow wide, their jaw drops, and they lean way back in shock. Some people will even go as far as to tell you that they feel sorry for you.

This is what it is like for me to also tell people that I never said the word, "Daddy," during my childhood. Someone who has had a present father all of their lives will wonder how I could live a life like that, but just like the seafood allergy – you can't miss what you have never had. I have been allergic to seafood from birth, so I never got the chance to discover how wonderful the food would taste in my mouth, much like the word, "Daddy".

For reasons outside of his control, I was never able to call out for my own biological father while I was growing up. As much as my father wanted me, he was also absent for different reasons. At least having Reggie in my life, even though it wasn't until my teenage years, gave me the opportunity to know what it was like to be loved and protected by a man who had nothing but the best in mind for you.

Once I had my own job and my own money, around sixteen years old, I began to contact my little brother more often. I would send for him to come visit me, because his grandparents lived in a nice area and weren't as interested in making sure that we stayed in contact. Sometimes, we would talk about what had happened in our childhood, and how we ended up separated the way we did. I would tell him about what I knew about our mother, and what may have caused her to choose the path that she did.

#DisableYourLabels

CHAPTER TWO
A Motherless, Fatherless Child

"Don't forgive him. Forgive yourself for believing there is something lacking in you because he wasn't there."

- Iyanla Vanzant

Levertry Sanders, aka Vert, was the starting basketball player for East Tech High School. He was tall, athletic, and handsome, and he knew it. Vert was a senior who was raised in the projects of Cleveland, Ohio, where life was literally do or die. He was also the man who would be my father.

Growing up in the projects was a matter of survival of the fittest on a daily basis. The presence of pistols, knives, fights, and shootings was the norm. Many of the people who found themselves in that place didn't find their way out of it, at least not alive. The familiar saying, "The good die young", took on a whole other meaning there, where you were lucky to see the age of twenty-one without being locked up or taken out in a body bag.

A common question to be asked in the projects when someone met you for the first time was, "who yo' people?" In other words, who vouching for you, because everybody knows everybody and we don't do unfamiliars. You are born there, you live there, and you die there. Your name meant something. Your family name meant even more. Your mother and father also lived there and died there, and most likely, your grandparents did, too. It was a given. There are three to five generations of families being raised in the projects, and no one is questioning why they haven't moved away yet. As I was growing up, I did not know that this was not normal for everyone else in the world. That dysfunction was normal to me. It's just the way it was.

The projects were arranged like a bunch of older, poorly-maintained brick homes, all in a row. They were built so close together that everyone had no choice but to know each other. Each day would be filled with the sounds of neighbors hanging their clothes out on clothes lines right next to each other while discussing the day's gossip, last night's lottery numbers, and who had died or went to jail. Even grass knew better than to grow in the projects. There weren't any porches or backyards to play in, and they didn't bother with steps or stairs, you just walked right on up to the front door.

Donna King couldn't have been more different than my father. She was raised on the "right side of the tracks". In fact, they would often call my mother the Black White Girl. She was the head cheerleader for John Adams High School, my father's rival team. She was also a senior, and she loved to sing and later even formed a band with her best friend, my Aunt Jean. She was proper and articulate, and until she met Vert, she had never stepped foot into the projects.

Vert had a greenish-colored Nova, and he would ride Donna around in it everywhere. Sure, blueish smoke would blow out from his tailpipe whenever he revved the engine, but my mother would later relay to me that no matter how dangerous the community that he lived in truly was, she never felt safer than when she was sitting by his side. My father just had that way about him.

One day, Donna and Vert were upstairs playing spades at Vert's mother's house, and Vert ran to answer the phone. The next thing she knew, his frantic screams erupted from downstairs and echoed throughout the house. Donna jumped up and rushed to the source of the commotion. She found him buckled up on the ground, clutching the telephone in his shaking fist.

"She's gone!" He bellowed.

"Who?" Donna gasped, frightened to see Vert in such a state of panic.

"Ann! Ann! She's gone!" Vert shook his head.

Ann, who was Vert's baby sister, had been shot and brutally murdered. As she sat in a parked vehicle with a man that would never be identified, he shot her and threw her body out of the car. Later, Vert's very own father, who we called Sugar Ray due to his proven skills at boxing (*he had them hands*), would come to realize that he had been walking past the scene of the crime precisely when his own daughter was being killed, but at the time, he did not know that it was Ann in the car. Keeping with the code of honor in the streets, "hear no evil and see no evil," and he continued walking with his eyes forward and his head down. Most likely, being an older gentleman, he wouldn't have been able to save her even if he *had* known, but he definitely would have tried. That knowledge would haunt him for the rest of his own life.

She was only nineteen years old at the time, and Ann left three young children behind to be raised without their mother in that cold and heartless place. Vert's mother, Madea, wasn't having that. Shortly thereafter, she moved the family out of the projects and into a home where Ann's three boys would be cared for without the threat of violence hanging over their heads constantly.

As I grew up, I remember that my mother used to say something to me all of the time about Ann. I obviously never got a chance to meet her in person, but I always heard such amazing compliments being given to her.

"Oh, Ann? Yes, she was a *baaad* woman! I mean, beautiful."

"Just gorgeous," family members would say.

My mother had her own way of telling me about Ann, though.

"Oh, yes. You actually look like your Aunt Ann. She was dark-skinned with beautiful white teeth. She was built like a brick house. Curvy. Really pretty," she would begin. I remember swelling with pride and grinning from ear to ear.

"Yep. You sure do look like her. Gonna end up just like her, too."

Through all of the tragedy that had befallen the family, Donna and Vert's relationship blossomed. They turned toward one another during the hard times. Although they faced ups and downs like any other relationship, their unique bond kept them returning to one another. In their case, opposites definitely attracted. However, one constant point of contention between the two of them was my mother's involvement in the band that she was in with Aunt Jean. Vert wasn't interested in the band, but he supported her nonetheless, being sure to be in the front row at every show. He would even take her back and forth to all of her rehearsals, until one night he didn't.

Vert couldn't see the value in putting so much effort into the rehearsals and practicing to go on tour. Although he admired her beautiful voice, he wanted to become a man of his own household. His charisma was setting him up for success in the neighborhood. He was making important connections.

As a natural born hustler, Leverty became a jack of all trades (but master of none.) Although he did attend Central State College, he didn't get to complete his time there. Fiercely intelligent, Vert enjoyed the gift of gab. He never knew a stranger.

#DisableYourLabels

Everyone knew that Vert was the life of any party. The festivities didn't start until he showed up, flashing that brilliant smile and greeting everyone like they were his best friend. My father knew how to speak to the smallest person in the room and somehow make them feel like the biggest.

This particular combination of talents would eventually be my father's downfall. The year was 1981. People who were close to Vert started to take notice of a change in his appearance and mannerisms.

"Vert, where you get all that money from?" His friends and family began to ask, after seeing him pull out stacks of money.

Suddenly, Levertry Sanders had access to things that a young Black man in Cleveland, Ohio wasn't used to having. He would begin to give Donna expensive gifts, like real diamond rings and fur coats. His intelligence was to be admired, and it was alleged that the mob had taken notice. This was an intense time for the organized crime scene and prominent families that were taking over power in the city. Vert's specific set of skills would have been much desired by certain people for certain tasks.

It was a hot and muggy evening in the middle of July.

The night that my father died, he had taken my mother to rehearsal for the last time. They argued like cats and dogs all the way there. Vert wanted Donna to quit the band for good, settle down with him, and start a family. They had already graduated high school three years before this conversation, and he was ready to be a family man. He was finding a great level of success and financial stature lately, and he wanted to share that with her.

Donna tried to explain to Vert that singing and performing was her passion. She wanted to tour and travel the country, and the last thing on her mind was settling down with children! When they got to the rehearsal site, Donna hopped out of the car in a huff, slamming the door behind her. The look on my father's face was pure anger and frustration as he sped away in a cloud of blue exhaust. My mother would tell me this story with tears threatening to escape her eyes, and she always ended it by saying, "There are some moments in life that you will never forget, and that is a memory that will haunt me for the rest of my life, daughter."

That night's rehearsal was as jovial as usual. It was full of fun, music and laughter, and the band ended their session cutting up and joking with one another until suddenly, the telephone rang. Aunt Jean says that she will never forget receiving that horrible phone call. She hung up the phone in silence and slowly walked towards my mother, wondering how it would be possible to tell her this devastating news.

"Donna, have a seat. I gotta tell you something, and it's going to hurt when you hear it," she said.

My mother looked at Jean in confusion. They had just been laughing and joking moments earlier, and now Jean looked like she was on the verge of crying. Her face looked ashen, as if she had seen a ghost.

"I don't know how to tell you this, but Vert is dead." Aunt Jean spoke in the calmest, softest tone that she could muster without bursting into tears herself. She braced herself for my mother's reaction.

"WHAT?! DEAD?! Naw, you got that wrong. I just saw Vert. He just dropped me off not even an hour ago! That can't be right. They must have the wrong person. Let me call Madea." She shook her head in disbelief and headed over to the phone.

As soon as Madea answered the phone, Donna could hear the pain in her voice.

"NO! MRS. SANDERS! NO!" My mother screamed into the phone.

"Yes, Donna… it's true," Madea answered, without ever hearing the question neither one of them could bear to be spoken.

"No. I just saw him an hour ago! No! No! NO!" My mother continued repeating over and over again, as if this chant would magically bring my father to life again.

The headlines would read that Leverty Sanders was murdered in cold blood by a gunshot wound to the head. He was a young black male, only twenty-two years of age, and even to this day, no one has ever been arrested for this heinous crime that would cause a devastating ripple effect throughout our family for decades to come.

My mother often would say that she believes in her heart that my father's charisma and outgoing character may have cost him his life. She would say that maybe he knew too much, that people had started trusting him with too much information, or that perhaps he was asked to do something that he refused to do. The thing is, when you work for The Mob, you do what you're told, repeat nothing you see or hear, and no matter what, ALWAYS stay loyal to the soil. Regardless of why it happened, it happened, and none of us would ever be the same again. In fact, the ripple effect would change my family from that moment on.

That open wound would never heal in my mother's heart. Each time she replayed in her mind the last time she saw my father, the one true and genuine love that she would ever have in her life, she would only remember that they were arguing and feuding. Donna would never get that chance to make up with him, to kiss him, and hear his laughter as he told her that he still loved her and just wanted to be with her forever and have her raise his children in their home together. To add insult to injury, she would find out weeks after his brutal death that she was pregnant with me.

A deep depression engulfed my mother after she found out that she was now a statistic, left to raise a fatherless baby without the man that died the same day that he pleaded with her to settle down and have his children.

"It doesn't seem right. How could God do this to me?!" Donna would cry out, day after day, until finally, Aunt Shirley had had enough.

"Honey, you are pregnant. Everything that you feel, that baby feels. What you go through, that baby inside of you goes through. Why don't you come live with me?"

Aunt Shirley knew what my mother had been through during her relatively short life. My mother's mother had passed away suddenly just one month after giving birth to her tenth child. My mother was the oldest of those ten children, and at the young age of eleven, she was tasked with the job of helping my grandfather raised her nine younger siblings. She might not have been there to raise my brother and me during most of our lives, but she sure did her share of mothering while she was yet a child herself. Whether she wanted to or not, she wasn't given much of a choice in the matter. It was a matter of necessity.

Now pregnant and feeling utterly alone, she needed support in every possible way. Aunt Shirley knew that during my mother's own childhood, she never had a real female role model around except for her grandmother, "Gran".

Gran was a full-fledged Indian, and this was before the politically-correct term of Native American was formed, and when she passed, my mother felt like she had lost her best friend. Aunt Shirley recognized that this was an opportunity for her to step up in a major way for my mother.

Aunt Shirley did everything in her power to make sure that Donna delivered a beautiful, healthy baby girl, and nine months later, that is just what she did. Aunt Shirley would be the one who would name me. She was the very first person to hold me, and she was the one who cut my umbilical cord.

When my mother first brought me home from the hospital, she didn't have the money to afford a crib, so she decorated a drawer right next to her bed and wrapped me up tight to sleep. I never left her side. Little did we know it then, but that was the most time that I would spend at my mother's side being nurtured by her.

#DisableYourLabels

About six months after I was born, my mother quit the band, remembering my father's last request of her. Her dreams of being an international professional singer went up in a cloud of smoke, as she began to feel that she had to sacrifice her own life for mine. Because of this deep-seated resentment, I often still wonder if my mother even likes me, although I know that deep down, she loves me. Being a young mother wasn't easy for her, taking on one menial job after another to provide for me.

A couple of years after my father's death, my mother hooked up with an old friend and wound up pregnant again this time giving birth to a baby boy. I considered my baby brother to be my own personal baby, and it was my job to protect him at all cost, even though I was only a couple of years older than him. The pressure of now having two young children to raise as a single mother dealing with her own depression and sadness was too much for her to bear. As so many people do, who are facing an overwhelming amount of adversity in their lives, she turned towards the numbing comfort of illicit drugs during this time, and that is how my brother and I ended up separated from each other years later. That was an incredibly jarring experience for so many reasons, but to understand how painful it really was, you would have had to understand our relationship.

Wherever I went, my brother went. If I slept, my brother slept. If you saw me, you would see him. I was his protector, and I loved him dearly. I still do. Before we could blink on that fateful Sunday that Mommy disappeared, we were torn from one another and forced to live apart for the rest of our lives. Since we've grown up and reconnected, we are still working to re-establish that relationship; but I often wonder who we would have been if my mother had made another choice on that day. Instead, I lost the closeness with my little brother during the most crucial part of our childhood, and I was made into a motherless, fatherless child at only five years old.

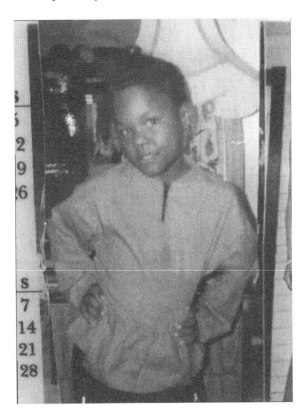

CHAPTER THREE

A Setback or A Setup for Your Future?

"You're never going to be able to control the environment, but you can control the way you react to it."

– Alison Levine

ecently, I was invited to speak at a high school in Las Vegas because the staff and teachers felt that the students were uncontrollable. They were at their wits end about what other recourse they could employ to take back their authority. They had been catching kids smoking weed and having sex under the bleachers. There was even a handful of young ladies caught giving oral sex in the boy's bathroom; my heart sank when they told me this. The staff felt that what the kids really needed was some *real* talk in a major way from someone that they could relate to and understand, but maybe, more importantly, someone who understood them. The entire 9th grade was in attendance when I showed up that day. I began to share with them what life was like for me when I was their age, and it wasn't anywhere near what they expected to hear.

My friends and I started off as "Cory Girls", which is what everyone referred to you as, if you played sports at the Cory Recreation Center on the corner of 105th Street and Drexel. We would hang out at the rec center during the summers and afterschool. They offered seasonal sports, like basketball, softball, and volleyball to give kids like us an outlet to have some sort of relief from the negative environment in which we were living. We were great at pretty much anything that we put our hands to, and we chose to put our hands towards beating all of the other teams on a regular basis.

I was also the captain of the cheerleading squad for the East 97th Street Bulldogs, which was a Muni League. Just like everything else in our community, there was an emphasis on which street or which block you were from. Everything came down to where you lived and you repped that street with your life. It was unusual for someone to be a Cory Girl *and* a Bulldog, because those weren't areas that necessarily got along with each other. But no one ever said that I was usual.

We were using these affiliations and sports teams to escape the grim reality that we were facing at home, where we slept two on a bed, it was one at the foot and one at the head. We would sleep with our shoes on and tied tight, and you had better sleep light. You literally never knew which family friend or relative would try to steal the Jordans right off your feet while you slept. This was a world where you would celebrate getting a new toy or gift at Christmas, and the next day wonder where that toy went because someone had made sure that if it had any value at all on the street, they were going to take it. The crazy part about it was that sometimes the same person who gave it to you would steal it from you to sell and get money for their next fix.

Most people don't really know about that life. They act like they do, in order to profit from making a rap album about it, sit around and joke about it, or create fake reality TV shows about it, but they have never actually lived it. They don't know anything about having the gas turned off by the gas company for non-payment, so you would turn the oven on and leave the door open to heat the entire house. They couldn't tell you anything about boiling water in pots and pans to be able to take a bath. Do you know how many pots it takes to fill up a bathtub? In my house, it was thirteen! Have you ever taken bread, poured sugar on top of it, and called it a sugar sandwich? That was considered breakfast on many days. Arguing and fighting amongst ourselves was a regular occurrence, so much so, that if it was quiet, you knew one of two things. Either no one was home, or something crazy was about to happen.

I never knew that people who didn't grow up in the same neighborhood that I did weren't going through the same things in their life. Being a six-year-old child and being sent to the corner store with a hand-written note telling the cashier to let you buy the cigarettes for a relative was perfectly normal to us. Most of us grew up with parents who were either dead, in jail, or addicted to drugs. More often than not, we were being raised by grandparents, aunts, great aunts, or older siblings, if you were lucky. If you weren't lucky, then being brought up in juvenile detention centers, half-way houses, group homes, or just being lost in the system would be your fate.

#DisableYourLabels

There are few experiences that are as gritty and stark as being a small child and walking to elementary school past crack houses and down dark alleys. How does one maintain healthy childhood innocence while stepping across crack pipes, used condoms, empty beer bottles, bullet shell casings, and various forms of drug paraphernalia? Or you waking up on a dirty mattress next to a baby who has had on the same soiled diaper for days and has a runny nose and dirty face, while you try to get yourself ready to go to class and still feel excited about learning. On your way out of the front door, with not a single morsel in your empty stomach, you'd feel a familiar crunch underneath your feet. It would be the rough, brown tobacco contents from the cigars that had been poured out in order to be refilled with marijuana and other drugs. It could also be the leftover black 'n' mild cigar tobacco that didn't make it back into the cigar after you "freaked it". How do you stay in the right frame of mind to grow, thrive, and obtain an education in such conditions?

At the age of seven years old, I could already identify what type of high a person had just by watching their mannerisms. Seeing the look in their eyes after they'd taken that hit, being able to see them begin to start chasing that high right in front of your face told you everything you needed to know. Children often see and understand more than we give them credit for, and in that dreary place, the things that children knew would shock you.

To give you an example, if someone had recently smoked some weed, they would be calm and mellow with red eyes that could barely even open, so their eyes looked almost slanted. You could expect them to raid the nearly empty refrigerator about an hour later to look for food once they got the munchies and got hungry. They'd laugh at the stupidest things, or they'd babble on and on about nothing, all the while thinking that they were the smartest person on earth.

But it gets worse – much worse. Crack was a very different type of high. Even though it is hard to explain, a child would know the signs when they saw them. They would recognize the familiar smell that would suddenly waft up from a bathroom, like a mix of burning rubber tires and black licorice. There would be thick smoke, no matter how hard they tried to stuff towels underneath the door to block it, because the person who was using couldn't stop themselves from taking a hit and then immediately opening that door to come out to inspect the rest of the house. They would hold their dried out, chapped lips a certain way when they'd talk, sort of pursed and to the side, like they'd just eaten a sour lemon. When someone has been smoking crack, they'd have a habit of grinding their teeth together without realizing it. Their eyes would be wide, darting from right to left, hearing and seeing things no one else could.

#DisableYourLabels

You could watch them continuously walk to the window, paranoid while looking out to see if someone was coming. They'd stare out of the peep hole in the front door for minutes on end, and they'd swear they heard police sirens when none were actually there. Sometimes, if they had been on a long run, smoking for a long time, they'd even start to hallucinate and see "shadow people" tormenting them in every darkened corner. Just when it seems like they might really start panicking, they'd dash back into the bathroom, lock the door behind themselves, and start the agonizing process all over again. Once their supply runs out, that person would do nearly anything to find more. There is a reason why people who have been blessed enough to overcome a crack addiction will often be heard saying, "One hit is too many, and a million hits will never be enough."

A heroin high constituted a totally different monster. Someone high on heroin would nod off and fall asleep right in the middle of their conversation with you, then moments later, they would pop back into reality and continue their sentence as if nothing had ever happened. Sometimes, that little nap could last several minutes! They would dance to music that wasn't playing, and their actions would just be random and out of the blue. Again, I ask, how does a child witness all of this on a regular basis at home, where it is supposed to be a safe sanctuary for them, and then function normally in school? I'd love to hear someone give me a real answer to that question.

The neighborhood was so small that if you did have a parent who was strung out on drugs, there was a good chance that it was someone you knew who was selling it to them. As crazy as it sounds, it would help keep the money flowing right in the community. As you grew older, you probably would be sitting in class with the person who was selling your mother drugs. You didn't think badly of them, or if you did, you didn't say so. They were just supplying a demand. If they didn't do it, someone else would, so you just learned to accept it. It's just the way it *was*.

Once you did get out of your home and started the trek towards school, there were even more challenges. We would often walk in packs through abandoned fields trying to get an education, where there was no telling who had been there the night before and what they had left behind for you to find. Depending on what they had used to party with and get high on, you could encounter just about anything during that journey. The same things that would shock a child growing up outside that area were just commonplace to us.

Just going through that area would put you in danger, because you would be walking through the rival territory of another neighborhood. That would usually mean that you would literally have to fight your way across it. On the West Coast, many people are familiar with the gang affiliations that involve colors, like the Crips (who would wear blue) and the Bloods (who would wear red). In my hood, it wasn't about what color you were wearing. It was about what street you were on and what hood you claim. So, if you had to go through an area to get to where you were trying to go, and it wasn't your hood and you had no homies on that block, you had no choice but to fight. That was why we traveled in packs, and we stayed ready for that action at the drop of a hat!

Often, those fights would follow you to school. You were fighting on the way to school. You were fighting once you got to school, and guess what? You were fighting once you get home after school too. A child growing up facing that stress daily cannot possibly then be expected to go to school, sit in a classroom, and follow the roles and expectations set forth by the teachers and administration without some sort of hitch. There is going to be some friction at some point, and behavior problems were more than common. How could there not be?

Coping with the suffocating lifestyle we were forced to face wasn't a choice. It was a matter of survival, and when it's a matter of survival, you do what you have to do – by any means necessary. We never thought long-term, and we never had the ability to try and develop an exit strategy. We never thought about the fact that we would one day be adults ourselves with children, and that it would then be our responsibility to teach and guide their futures. It was a matter of life and death in those streets. I couldn't see myself making it to the age of sixteen, let alone eighteen and beyond. You just did what you had to do to make it to the next day. Surviving into adulthood was an exception, not an expectation.

Those coping skills would stay with me, even to this day, and they have been vital in helping me to get to where I am now. You see, I understand these children that I address at these speaking engagements, and I understand that this is precisely why I can be someone that can make a difference. It is far easier to judge someone when you have not walked a mile in their shoes. I have walked that mile and then some, fighting my way through the whole time.

DISABLE YOUR LABELS
What does your future look like?

I like to share with my audiences something I call the GPS Theory. In order to operate a GPS, you must start out with two things. You must know where you are right now and most importantly, you must know where you want to be! Growing up, all we knew was that we wanted to stay alive. What good is a GPS with no destination set? Would you board an airplane with no destination? Your mind is your GPS but many of us are living day to day with no plans of where we want to go. Even the Bible says, "Better is the end of a thing than the beginning thereof." We all have a past, and that is something that you cannot change or alter, but have you ever taken a moment to really think about what your future could look like? Better yet, what do you *want* it to look like? Most people have a tendency to hide behind their past, or even their current situation, using it as an excuse for why they haven't been able to make it in life.

It's easy to give a hundred reasons why we *can't*. Now is the time to give yourself just *one* reason why you *can!* I know it's not easy. I'm not claiming that it was. My Aunt Shirley would say, "You can't see the forest for the trees." In other words, don't be so caught up with all of your problems that it becomes so overwhelming you can't see the solution that is right in front of you. Adjust your vision, and see your way out. Do not live in the past. Let me tell you, do not let your past come to your present and destroy your future. If God can forgive and forget your past, then so can you! According to 2 Corinthians 5:17, "Therefore if any man be in Christ, he is a new creature: old things are passed away; behold, all things are become new."

Look, I know what it's like to want to make something out of nothing. I know about survival. I definitely know what it's like to come from a dysfunctional home, having an absent parent who is either dead, incarcerated, or addicted to drugs. I experienced all three scenarios before the age of ten. However, I had two choices. Would I allow those things to be the reason that I would fail, or would I make those things be the reason that I was *fueled?*

Education is the great equalizer. A doctor is not born saving lives. They are educated for many years on how to treat people. One thing that I did realize at a young age was that I needed to teach myself how to be book smart and street smart at the same time – no excuses. Your environment does not define you, and if I can make it out of hell, so can you. Educate yourself, have a vision for your life, and a plan to get there, even if you get knocked off course, keep going, keep growing! Let's be honest, we all have made a wrong turn while using our GPS and what happened? The GPS said "rerouting". Listen once you have the destination. The creator of the universe, God will get you there. Even if you make a mistake or go the wrong way, you can still be turned around. Bad relationships, failing grades, incarceration, not listening to teachers, parents, and adults these are wrong turns, but they can be turned around if you understand you want to get somewhere further than where you are right now. Trust me you have the power, you have the right, you have the choice to live your dream life. It will take listening, discipline, hard work, and sacrifice to get there, but it can and will be gone if you don't give up.

What is your own exit strategy? We all have what we define as our own type of "normal". For so many of us, including myself, dysfunction is our normal. The way I grew up, my normal was not the average person's normal, but that didn't stop me. I am in no way saying that this life that I was forced to live is okay in no way, shape, form, or fashion. What I *am* saying is that many of our youth today are also growing up this way, and until you have had to face the same circumstances, it is very hard to say what you would or wouldn't do.

Like anyone else, it hurts my heart to hear of a beautiful fourteen-year-old girl giving away the most precious parts of her body because she was never told that her body is a jewel, not a tool. Because every TV show, Influencer, song, and Reality show, is telling her that sex sells and she believes it. It brings tears to my eyes to know that the only male role model that many of these young men will see are gangsters, drug dealers, drug users, rapists and killers because their fathers are not around to teach them any differently, or worse yet – their fathers are one of the above.

If you are currently living within a dysfunctional situation, whatever that may be; I am challenging you to begin to move in the right direction by asking yourself a few questions so you can create a new normal. What is your plan to get out? Where do you want to be in two years, five years, or even ten? These are questions I never had the luxury of asking myself at a young age when it would have been crucial to do so. What is your current plan of action? In other words what must you do each day to get you closer to where you want to be? Now, think about what you currently do each day. Are your daily activities if you wrote them all down, getting you closer to where you want to be, or pushing you even farther away?

It is easier for us to concentrate on the present, because it is right there in front of us. What can you do today to begin to, instead, plan for the future? What steps are you willing to take to start to change your future and not continue to live in the past?

When people ask me how I survived the situation I was brought up in – and not just survive, but how did I end up being able to *thrive* – I have to explain that even though I didn't realize it at the time, the things that I did between the ages of thirteen and sixteen years old would help to shape my future. Those things may not have seemed like healthy and positive choices at the time, but they allowed me to build a foundation for success that pushed me to where I stand today. You work with what you are given, and then you use it to create what you desire. Despite setback after setback, I persevered, and that is what I am asking you to do. It may seem easier said than done, but I did it with the right formula. Before I go into what that formula was, I need to reveal one of the biggest trials that I encountered at the tender age of sixteen that nearly knocked me off my path.

CHAPTER FOUR
The F- Word That Changed My Life

"A warning always comes before the storm."
- *Dorothy Sanders, my grandmother*

One of the happiest moments in my life happened in 2014 when I was blessed to be able to attend "The Life You Want Tour" hosted by Oprah Winfrey. I can remember her saying that you should always listen to the whisper. God will speak to you in a whisper at first, hoping to get your attention. Now, if you don't listen to the whisper, your situation will develop into a problem. If you continue to ignore the new problem and stubbornly go about your own way, next, you will experience a catastrophe.

Have you ever felt overwhelmed by your circumstances? Have you ever looked up to the sky and asked yourself, "Why me? How did this happen to me?!" What if I told you that all of the signs were there to show you what was to come, way before any of it ever happened?

I can remember being sixteen years old back in 1998. Only two more years of high school and I would be done! I was never your average sixteen-year-old girl. Even then, I was all hips and butt, with small breasts, a flat stomach, and snatched tight in the waist. Being blessed with flawless dark skin, bowed legs, a bright white smile that would light up a room – I thought I was ready for the world.

Attending Cleveland School of the Arts (CSA), I recall riding the public city bus to school every morning. The guy who sat across from me caught my eye. We always got off at the same stop, but I knew that I had never seen him walking around my campus. I came to find out that he was going to the college that was right across the street from my own high school.

One day, he finally approached me. He told me that he was a freshman, and I reasoned that this wasn't so bad. There was only a two-and-a-half-year difference between us. The friends from my neighborhood caught wind of the two of us talking, and all they could say was, "Wow! You met someone in *college?*" You need to understand that going to college wasn't even on our radar as only 2 out of every 10 of us even graduated high school, and dating someone who was going to college was completely unheard of!

We hit it off immediately. Soon, we were on the phone on a daily basis for hours on end. I'd laugh at all of his jokes, and he got all of mine. It was a struggle to finally hang up late at night.

"You hang up first," he said softly.

"No, you hang up."

"I miss you," he told me.

"I miss you more!" I sighed.

He'd tell me about his experience in college, and I would listen intently, soaking in every word. He was frustrated with the way he was being treated unfairly by his professors simply because he was a young Black man. He'd reveal his dreams of owning his own business one day, and I could feel my heart swelling. I'd never heard anyone talk like this before. I was intrigued. I had never known a man like him.

I'd never been so mentally stimulated by someone before. I thought that I was in Heaven, finally finding someone outside of my own neighborhood. He stopped taking the bus one day, informing me that he had gotten his own car. We were both so excited to finally be able to go on a real date.

I was so excited to tell my home girls, and they were just as excited for me.

"Tell us about your date when you get back, girl!" This was before we were able to do things like post selfies, check in to places that we visited, or give minute-by-minute status updates via social media. My friends would have to wait to hear from me on their home phones, two-way pagers, or beepers to get the 411 on what had happened during my amazing night.

He picked me up and even opened the car door for me like a gentleman. That was all new to me. No one had ever opened a car door for me in my life. We pulled up to a house, and I was under the impression that it was his mother's home. I was all smiles as he came around and let me out. When we walked in, I was perplexed to hear excruciatingly loud music blaring, and two dudes yelling excitedly at each other as they played a video game on the couch in the living room.

"Is this your mom's place?" I asked timidly, struggling to be heard over the bass booming from the stereo system.

"Naw baby, it's my cousin's house. Don't worry. I got you."

I began to get uncomfortable. This was not what we had talked about. An uneasy feeling began creeping its way up my spine.

"I thought we were going to…" I stammered.

"Baby, my cousin's house was closer. It's cool. I said I got you. We are going to my house later." He shrugged off my concerns nonchalantly.

This was the first sign that I would hear Oprah speak about so many years later. This was God whispering into my spirit that something just wasn't right. I knew that this turn of events was not okay, but I was eager to please this man who had captured my young girl's heart. I followed him further into the house.

He suggested that we go upstairs to get away from all of the music and so that we could hear each other speak without shouting. My feet felt as heavy as lead as I dragged them up those stairs reluctantly. Here was phase two, where the whisper morphed into a problem, and I didn't even realize that it was happening! *He would never let anything bad happen to you. It's been six months, and he's always had your back. You're in good hands, girl. Stop tripping;* I continued to repeat to myself. Each step felt like it took a day to ascend. My neck started to grow warm, and my palms began to sweat. I tried to control my anxiety, not wanting to seem like I was acting like a baby with this grown man. I continued to attempt to silence my inner intuition. I didn't want to cause any problems or make him feel like I was being difficult. The last thing that I wanted was for him to assume that I didn't trust him. He was supposed to be my man.

Once we got upstairs, he led me into a small bedroom and gestured for me to sit on the small twin-sized bed. He turned on the television, and we sat quietly semi-watching it. I was a ball of nerves, but I still tried to conceal how I was feeling by flashing my famous hundred-megawatt smile. He leaned over and began kissing me aggressively, like he had never done before. We had never been in a situation like this, where we could be alone with no one watching us.

His hands began to roughly wander over my shoulders, down my arms, and towards my waist. I leaned back from his kiss, and said gently, trying to remain as un-argumentative as possible, "No, I'm not ready for that yet, baby."

He knew that I was still a virgin. I had never had sex before, and I sure didn't want my very first time to be in some random house on an itty-bitty bed with some boring television show as background music and the voices of a bunch of loud people yelling downstairs. I didn't even know if they were aware that this was what he had planned when he brought me here.

"C'mon," he urged impatiently, proceeding to lean in and started kissing me on my neck once again as if I hadn't just told him no, "Don't you love me? I mean, I love you, and we gonna be together forever, right? You know you're my future wife, so what does it matter if we have sex now or later?"

"Yes, it does matter! Can you just take me home?" I pulled away. Little did I realize that phase three was swiftly barreling towards me like a runaway train – the catastrophe was just around the corner.

The look that came across his face and into his eyes is one I will never forget. It was as if a totally new person took over the body of the person that had gradually captured my heart for the past few months. His eyes were bloodshot red, and the veins in his neck and forehead bulged out of his skin frighteningly. To say that he seemed angry would be a huge understatement.

"You said you *loved* me!" He began to call me every name in the book besides my own. He was furious, and I was terrified. I tried to reason with him, pleading for him to calm down and take it easy. At first, I had tried to somehow salvage this date. This was supposed to be a beautiful night. We were supposed to be celebrating his new car. I thought I was meeting his mother for the first time. It was supposed to be a big milestone in the most meaningful relationship I had experienced in my young life, and now it had quickly transformed into a nightmare.

Once I realized that saving the night was impossible, I started to try and concentrate on just getting out of there and keeping myself safe. I got up from the bed and began to slowly back away from him, still trying unsuccessfully to calm him down. He stalked closer and closer to me; spit flying from his lips as he unleashed another string of profane words at me. Before I knew it, my back hit a wall, and I dejectedly realized that I had managed to back myself into a corner – figuratively and literally. There was nowhere to go, and he was between me and the door.

He reached out with both hands, gripping me harshly by my shoulders and flinging me back onto the bed. I began to kick and scream, hoping someone would hear me through all of the noise and music. I cried out for help, but help never came. I still wonder to this day if the people downstairs heard me and didn't choose to come, or if they never heard me at all. Hot tears flowed so heavily from my eyes that my vision was blurry. I fought for my life, but every punch, kick, and attempt to hurt him didn't seem to have any effect.

My mother's voice suddenly rang out in my head, "Save yourself for that special man. Make sure it's special. Your very first time should be a night to remember." Unfortunately, it would be, but for all of the wrong reasons. I felt that I was disappointing her.

As I struggled against him, he responded by choking me so hard that I felt that I would pass out. My body eventually sagged underneath him due to exhaustion and the lack of oxygen. An indescribable pain erupted below my waist, and I knew in that moment that the unforgettable experience that I had been waiting to have with that special man was now gone forever. It would never happen. I held my breath for what seemed like an eternity – but could have only been a few minutes – as he thrusted back and forth like a crazed person.

When it was all over, all that I could do was grab whatever clothing I could that were not ripped or covered in blood. I ran down the stairs, avoiding the eyes of anyone who may have been watching me, and out into the blinding sunlight.

Not only were all traces of innocence stolen from me that day, but so much more was lost. All of my hopes and dreams of finding a man who would treat me like a special queen and truly love me were left right there in that room. That was the longest bus ride that I have ever taken. I felt as if every person I walked past knew exactly what had happened when they caught a glimpse of how upset and disheveled I must have looked. Everyone on the street, in every car, at the bus stop, and on every corner seemed to be staring at me with judgement in their eyes.

I felt so betrayed. How had I let myself get played this way? I was smart. Not just book smart, but street smart. I was confused and hurt. How did this happen? I'd never felt so alone. I dedicated six months of my life to nurturing this relationship. To a young sixteen-year-old girl, that was like a decade – and for what? I even started questioning if his mother knew what type of boy she had raised?

To add insult to injury, when I finally got home, the phone wouldn't stop ringing. All of my friends wanted to know all of the details about how my first real date with the handsome college boy had went. They wanted all of the juicy news, and I couldn't blame them. I had hyped my home girls up, and now they needed the scoop.

#DisableYourLabels

Deep down, what they really wanted to know was, *what was it like to step outside of our bubble?* How did it feel to venture outside of our neighborhood? They needed to hear from me that it was possible for girls like us to find a quality man with a good job and a real education. They needed to know that they didn't have to settle for the thugs we grew up with who sold drugs or spent time in and out of jail. It was a huge cross to bear. What do I tell them? Do I tell the truth and get their love and support, but at the same time destroy their own hopes and dreams? Or do I take the harder route for myself and try to salvage their hopes that I no longer possessed? I took a deep breath, my hand clutching the phone tightly, and repeated over and over again to each one of my friends the same rehearsed line, "Girl, he just wasn't my type."

By myself in the bathroom, I thought that maybe if I took a hot enough shower, I could boil away the shame. Where I had previously loved the smell of his cologne, I now couldn't stand having this rapist's scent on me any longer. To this day, I still take extremely hot baths and showers.

I sat in my house for weeks, not wanting to socialize or do anything that I didn't have to do. I couldn't keep answering the questions. I never told a soul what happened to me, and the first time that I am talking about it is in the book you hold in your hands right now.

I failed to listen to my inner self when we arrived at the house. I continued to push aside the warning signals God had given me, and I could have very well paid with my life. And even though I blamed myself during that period wishing I had been stronger and more discerning; however, now that I am older and wiser, I realize for a fact that there was nothing that I could have done differently that day. I couldn't have really known how the chain of events would have played out, and I was a naïve teenager with wide eyes and a trusting heart.

It feels like I have replayed that day out in my mind a million times. Until something like that happens to you, which I sincerely pray it never does, you have no idea how you would really react in the situation. People may be thinking, *why didn't you call the police?* My answer to that is, what exactly would I have told them? The boyfriend that I thought I loved with all my heart just raped me? Should I have forced myself to answer their inevitable probing questions, like, "Did you agree to go inside the house with him? Did you go upstairs willingly with him? Did you sit on the bed with him? Did you tell him not to kiss you?"

I should've brought the police to my door, in my neighborhood, in front of my mother? Are you insane? What exactly was I supposed to tell my mother after all of those years of her and Buttercup telling me to make sure my first time was special? Maybe you were a different kind of sixteen-year-old girl who had the forethought and maturity to do something like that. I was not, and I did what I had to at the time.

I felt like such a failure. Never had I felt so powerless in my life. Everyone knew me as the confident one. I was the one always with a smile on my face. Now, I only felt alone. I felt like no one could possibly understand me or what I was going through. Even though men were constantly trying to still hit on me every day, I felt unattractive and ugly. My scars and scratches were healing on the outside, but the ones on the inside were just beginning to grow.

DISABLE YOUR LABELS
Stop giving your energy and power to people and things that don't deserve it!

How many of us are silently allowing others to take our power away? We have all encountered trials and tribulations that we had no control over at the time. They weren't our fault, and there was no way for you to change their outcomes. Allowing those people to continue to negatively affect your life and your personal success doesn't hinder that person who traumatized you. Trust and believe, *that* person is going on with their life just fine. It only obstructs you. It only delays *your* progress. You are giving that person permission to inhibit and impede your life over and over and over again!

What I have learned is a difficult word that people often hate to hear, love to receive, but struggle to give to others. Thankfully, I learned early that I would have to use this word often if I was going to get further in my life. I like to call it the F- Word! You have to F these people! That word is FORGIVENESS. Yes, forgiveness. It's important we forgive others for several reasons: 1) You reap what you sow if you forgive the day you need to be forgiving you will receive it. Even the Bible says in Matthew 6:14-15, " [14] For if you forgive other people when they sin against you, your heavenly Father will also forgive you. [15] But if you do not forgive others their sins, your Father will not forgive your sins." And 2) So you can move forward, let me explain.

I know that this is easier said than done. I know that people have played you, lied to and about you, and betrayed you. When they were supposed to love you, care for you, or even protect you. Still carrying anger, hate, and malice towards someone else in your heart creates dis-ease within your body. You are not at ease. You are troubled. This painful dis-ease then translates literally into a disease that will cause your body to express its unsettled and disturbed state in various ways, like ulcers, heart attacks, migraines, cancers, and much more. Your unwillingness to forgive people and certain past situations may be costing you more than you know. I'm not here to preach to you or to judge the way that you are coping with your own struggles, because this is an ongoing work in progress for us ALL. I am showing you what worked for me and many others. Forgive and move on for your own personal healing, not theirs. Only then will you see your true destiny come to fruition.

The acclaimed American inspirational author, Jonathan Lockwood Huie, who has been called the "Philosopher of Happiness", has an incredible quote that I have held near and dear to my heart. I would like to share it here with you. He says, "Forgive others not because they deserve it, but because you deserve peace."

This horrible experience that I went through, with someone I thought had my best interests at heart, could have been my undoing. If I would have let that prevent me from doing what I had to do, you wouldn't be reading this book right now. If that terrible moment years ago had hampered me from moving forward, I would never have been able to speak in front of massive audiences today and affect young lives. Instead, I found a way through all the pain and suffering. I moved past it to finally find my own greatness, the same way I believe that you are going to as well. Disable Your Labels of thinking: you're a victim but you are victorious because you overcame it. This book is to challenge you to think differently, the glass is not half empty but have full. You are worth reaching your dreams, you are worthy to have healthy relationships and friendships in your life, NEVER FORGET THAT! No matter what a past situation looks like, don't allow it to hinder you or keep you from true happiness, prosperity, joy, and love.

Also, if you are in a situation that is causing you pain, torment, disappointment, heartache, and headache, get out of that situation. The Bible says in Proverbs 10:22, "The blessing of the Lord, it maketh rich, and he addeth no sorrow with it." So, in other words, a blessing should not cost you your happiness, your peace of mind, your safety, or even your freedom. A situation shouldn't make you feel like you want to cry always sad, depressed, feel like you are not worthy, useless, or want to die. That's not the will of God for your life. You are worthy, you are amazing, uniquely made, and created for a purpose. The Bibles says in Jeremiah 29:11, "For I know the plans I have for you," declares the LORD, "plans to prosper you and not to harm you, plans to give you hope and a future." So, don't let anyone tell you you are meaningless, pointless; purposely, God said He know the plans He have for you and it's to prosper you and not to harm you. I just want to keep expressing God is not about you being harmed. Get away from those things, people, and situations that try to bring harm to you in any way. And remember to forgive, forget, and more importantly move on.

Ghetto Blues
Written by Desirae King
Age 17 years old

Verse 1

He was tall dark-skinned with pretty brown eyes
Sexy lips, kept a whip, and a mouth full of lies,
But still, he was the only man between these thighs,
I said, "I better be the only girl to make that thang rise!"
But you know a man do what he do, screw who he screw
And come home saying that he only loves you.
But I felt like I had to compete with you and the streets
You had broads paging you, waking me out my sleep.
Finally, I get you to see you only need me
Calling me ya wife saying one day I'd be.
You showed me pleasure during all my pain
No longer insane, no longer in vain
No lonely nights I'm screaming ya name.
Until the day they came and kicked the door down
Had a pistol at ya temple and had you on the ground
I just looked at the sky and said, "What to do now?"
Got me writing the man I love, like we f**king penpals!
After all this bullsh*t that I had to go through
Between the girls, the green, the fiends, the cops separated me from you
I guess I'll never win, I was bound to lose, Black woman of 2000 with these "Ghetto Blues"

THE F- WORD THAT CHANGED MY LIFE

Chorus
Hard times got me using my nine, not using my mind
I'm on the Fin- line, Mz. Fin, the front line not hard to find.
I'm out here trying to make ends meet, hustling in these streets,
and I'm playing for keeps.

Verse 2
On Feb 14th we buried Granny away
So how can I say "Happy Valentine's Day"?
You took the only person who told me to keep my head up
I didn't have nowhere to sleep she always kept a bed up
Man, I'm fed up with society and all these lies
All these broken promises and all these cries
She didn't see my 18th birthday before she died
Nine days away, I only look and ask God, "Why?"
Granny of the survivors and P.L.S, you know how we do
We put non-survivors in yo chest you know how we do
But even the thuggish gotta say, "I miss you!"
I wish it wouldn't have been you that got sent to the ground.
Man, I'm being selfish, 'cause you passed this wealth sh*t
You in a heavenly place where you're better dealt with, my heart
melt with
Memories, so when you see me think of Toot, Aunt Shirley, and of
course, my daddy,
And reppin' for my people from the f-i-v-e Nick, Net, Chris, D.A,
and of course, my granny.

Chorus
Hard times got me using my nine, not using my mind

#DisableYourLabels

I'm on the Fin- line, Ms. Fin, the front line not hard to find.
I'm out here trying to make ends meet, hustling in these streets,
and I'm playing for keeps.

CHAPTER FIVE

From Struggling to Success – The Insider's Formula

"When you want to succeed as bad as you want to breathe, then you'll be successful."

- Eric Thomas

When people hear my story and where I come from, they tend to tilt their heads to the side and look at me strangely. They see the woman that I am now – a motivational speaker, an author, a successful entrepreneur – and the question that I am most often asked is, "So, how did you get from *there* to *here?*" Reconciling the connection between the Desirae that lived that rough and grimy project life and the Desirae who now encourages and inspires others with her accomplishments is difficult in many people's minds. I believe that' the reason why there is such a disconnect because they don't realize that the division between that life and this one is not as wide as some may think. Same formula, different variables. Let me explain.

In high school, my home girls and I formed a clique that we called P.L.S., which stood for Pimpin' Ladies Style. Our block had become one of the most profitable ones in the city. East 105th Street (aka the 10-5, aka the 10-Fin) was poppin', and what had made it so popular could be summed up in one word – heroin. There were only three places in the entire city where you could cop heroin at that time, and we were one of them.

That particular drug was so hard to find back then because of the consequences that came with being caught with it. Your sentence was doubled if the drug that you happened to be selling was heroin, so most of the dope boys weren't touching it with a ten-foot pole. That meant that the people who were brave enough to risk it were in for a big payout, because it was definitely in high demand.

Maybe it was the poverty that made us so fearless. If you were broke, sometimes it felt like you were almost better off dead or in jail. Most of us came from homes with multiple children and single mothers. Government assistance like Section 8 housing, welfare, and food stamps or EBT cards was the norm; not the exception. Many of our mothers actually met and befriended each other while waiting in line at the government offices, the churches, rec centers or charities looking for assistance.

#DisableYourLabels

As the children who were the recipients of brown box lunches, holiday donations, and other people's hand-me-downs, we grew tired of getting left overs. We wanted more. We wanted our *own*. We were growing up in an environment where we would receive whatever someone else gave us, whether we liked it or not. It was common to hear, "That's dinner. You better eat all that food, and if you don't, oh well! You'll wait for the next meal."

It all began with the older teens and the young men in their twenties. All of a sudden, we were seeing them with new Jordans and Air Force One tennis shoes. In the wintertime came the fresh Timberlands Boots. If you had anything else on your feet, it was garbage. The men always had on Polo shirts, and their haircuts were fly. They had money in their pockets, and they ate whatever they wanted.

We had never seen people in our neighborhood have nice things like that. It's different when you see someone from a nice neighborhood across town flossing with their fancy clothes and car, but to see someone who lived next door to you with it? To see someone who you know goes to the same school you go to, or who you have seen grow up just like you have, walking around with new things that they bought with their own money? That was a different feeling, because I know that if *this person* can do it, then I know that I can do it. This is the basis for why I am so compelled to speak to people in the inner cities today. I need them to know that if I could make it out, so can they. Just because you are born into poverty doesn't mean you have to stay there. I need them to know that I am one of *them*.

East 105th Street had everything you could need from heroin to weed, between Kempton, Somerset, and South B. You would always find whatever it was that you were looking for. The code of honor between the dope boys was that if you sold crack, you stayed in your lane and in your own area. If you sold heroin, same thing. They didn't mix the two, and I couldn't really tell you why. It was all illegal anyway, so you wouldn't think that it would matter, but it did. The one exception was the weed man, who could travel between neighborhoods. Everybody needed a good weed man!

#DisableYourLabels

This is how I began to learn the formula for the success that would eventually catapult me right out of that lifestyle. My P.L.S. home girls and I were an anomaly. We were cool with everybody, and that meant we had access to *everything*. We had no fear, so selling drugs wasn't a problem. It was a means to an end. We were the only females willing to put in the work, so we could get it all. We were teenage females in the 90's. No one thought about messing with us. We grew up in this lifestyle. As I mentioned earlier, many of us had parents who were strung out on drugs, so what you didn't see in the street you saw at home anyway. Why wouldn't we take advantage of the fact that we were surrounded by the resources, and we could make real money selling the most highly demanded products in the city? To us, it was a win/win situation.

"Oh! You're under eighteen?" The old heads would say, "You good. You'll only go to juvey if you get caught. You're a minor. By the time you turn eighteen, that'll fall right off your record. It won't be on your *permanent* record." This was how they justified the risk that we were taking. Whether that was really true would remain to be seen, but it was enough explanation for us. In actuality, they were using us as bait. Our hunger for wanting to do something nice for ourselves drove us to do what we had to do.

Years later, we would come to find out that all of those empty promises of being safe from the long hand of the law were lies. If you ended up catching a federal case or being caught so many times that they began to call you a career criminal, the court would take all those things into consideration when they began sentencing you. If we had only known then what we know now, it might have made a difference. Those crimes most definitely *could* be placed on your permanent record, regardless of your younger age!

The summers were hot in Cleveland, Ohio. Daisy dukes and halter tops were our uniforms back then, and in the winters, we'd have snow up to our knees. It would be brutally cold, and white smoke would come from our mouths when we breathed. Nevertheless, we knew that if we were going to eat, we were going to have to get up and work. Our only option was to layer up – three pairs of socks, an undershirt, a t-shirt, a sweater, and a hoodie under your coat just to keep warm! Try to roll a blunt in zero-degree weather. Looking back, I don't know how we did it, but we did. It was really simple – how bad do you want to make this money? If you were hungry enough, you were going to make a way, and if you're lame enough, you would make an excuse, so which were you?

We'd risk our lives every single day just to get that money. Once we younger kids started to sell drugs, we also started going to jail. No one was teaching us the game; we were learning by trial and error. There was no manual to this thing. It took for some of us to start going to jail to learn how to hide the dope, how to look out for the cops, or what an undercover looked like. Some of us were getting eighteen months (which was a lifetime to us back then). A few of us got boot camp or the halfway house. Some of us were getting a slap on the wrist, and some were getting probation. It all depended on if you had priors and what type of lawyer you had.

Jay-Z once said in his song, *Never Change*, "It's cool to cop, but more important is lawyer's fees. That's how it is now. That's how it always be." If you had enough sense to put aside some money, you could get a good lawyer. Not all of us understood the importance of having a good lawyer.

Not everyone can handle going to jail. For those of us who couldn't, they started to put the dope down and started to pick the gun up instead "robbing". This was how the progression of crime evolved. They were tired of getting time for dealing drugs, so they'd rob the dope man. What was the dope man going to do if you robbed him? Call the police? Eventually, this was also how the murders began. The dope man would kill the robber for trying to rob him, or the robber would kill the dope man for not giving it up.

Between the police trying to arrest you, the fiends trying to play you, the robbers trying to rob you, your plug trying to give you some bad dope, and all the haters preying on your downfall, you always had to be on your A-game. We were lucky. Because we were cool with everyone, we had options. In the next chapter, I will go into how I got into the game initially, but for now, I want you to concentrate on seeing that there was a formula that we used to succeed back then, and it is the same formula that can be applied in any situation to succeed and "Disable Your Labels Financially."

As crazy as it sounds, even though we were using it to do illegal things, we began to formulate a plan on how to be successful doing what we were doing at the time, and we stuck to it. That is how we ended up making money and so, when my mother said to me, "My house, my rules..." At the age of eighteen, I decided that I needed my own place. I ended up with my own apartment downtown. I DIDN'T

WRITE THIS CHAPTER TO CONDONE SELLING DRUGS, I'M NOT SAYING IT'S OK TO ROB, NOR AM I SAYING KILLING IS OK!! I didn't write this chapter to give you a roadmap on how to do so, but instead, I want to share with you the experiences and life lessons that taught me how to get to where I am today.

DISABLE YOUR LABELS
Insiders Formula to Going from Struggling to Success

- Define the specific goals that you are trying to achieve right now.

You just need one goal to start off with, don't try to handle too much. Rome wasn't built overnight, but it was built brick by brick, (Buttercup used to always say that... lol). Back then, our number one goal was very clear: get enough money to support our lifestyle and survive. We just wanted nice clothes, shoes, and a decent meal. We stopped being the victim and became the victor. We took life into our own hands and created something out of nothing!

- Understand what is preventing you from accomplishing those goals and figure out ways to get around those obstacles.

Like I stated before, we were too young to get jobs back then, so illegal activities were all we could do in our eyes. There were several obstacles: the police, robbers, finding a reliable plug (supplier) but our thing was this, when it boils down to life or death, you choose life. When it boils down to feast or famine you choose feast. When you find an obstacle, you must realize it's not there to be a stumbling block, it's meant to be a stepping stone; it's all about perception.

- Determine what you are willing to sacrifice in order to successfully reach your desired objective.

We were willing to RISK OUR LIVES!!!! I'm NOT saying you should put your life in harm's way but rather, I'm saying, "What are you willing to sacrifice?" To be honest, we are all self-made but only the wealthy will admit it. That's why they call themselves "Self-Made Millionaires." Have you ever heard an employee say, "I'm a self-made employee?" No! We understood back then that we were completely in control of our lives. So, you must disable the label of: my boss, my parents, my kids, my employer put me in this situation. No, you are fully responsible for your life and the results that you have so far. We understood we had to be our own heroes & heroines and no one was going to fly through the air with a cape and thousands of dollars to save us from our poverty. Often, people get so caught up in blaming others that they forget to take full responsibilities for their own lives and the predicaments they are in.

- Decide what the reward will be when you reach your goal. What is the number one result or outcome you are looking for?

We were so focused on the outcome till we weren't concerned by the consequences or obstacles that stood in our way. Some people are so paralyzed by the obstacles they face on the way to success till they stop and get stuck right there. This points out to me that their WHY is not strong enough. In other words, the reason why they want to do something is not strong enough. A lot of times I see so many people blame others for their situations, when in truth, you can either focus on the problem or the solution, but you can't do both. You must become laser-focused and obsessed with the result/outcome you are looking to achieve and don't focus on anyone or anything else. Know the difference between attractions and distractions. Attractions are the things that are designed to get you closer to your desired results which may be camouflaged as an obstacle. Distractions are things that appear to be getting you to your desired results but in actuality taking you farther from it.

- Establish a crew. You must have people surrounding you with the same goals in mind, the same dreams, and who are headed in the same direction. You need a mastermind group.

Even Jesus had 12 disciples. Be not deceived, you can NOT do it alone. Even the Bible says in Genesis 11:6, "And the Lord said, Behold, the people is one, and they have all one language; and this they begin to do: and now nothing will be restrained from them, which they have imagined to do." Yes, there are some journeys you have to travel alone but you will need someone: teacher, coach, mentor, teammate, cheerleaders; someone to help you get through the rough times when you can't seem to find your way. No one person can do everything; so, find yourself a team of people that support your vision and goals similar to yours. THIS STEP WILL MAKE YOU OR BREAK YOU. You are only a direct reflection of the people YOU DECIDE to hang around with.

While I was growing up in high school, I had to show and prove how badly I wanted to make it. There weren't any excuses, and there couldn't be any fear. The P.L.S. girls walked with confidence where we needed to go, and once we got there, we did what we needed to do to make things happen. That is essentially the same thing that I do today. I walk into an event or a speaking engagement with confidence, and I make it happen wherever I go. That same business mind and work ethic has gotten me this far and it will take me even farther still.

It is so important to have good like-minded people around you. Birds of a feather flock together. If you take a look at the top five people in your life right now, the people who you see most often, interact with on a regular basis, even socialize with can go a long way in determining your future.

#DisableYourLabels

I guarantee that if your top five are filled with unhappy, complaining, and unsatisfied people, you will be one also, if you aren't already! If you hang out with five people who never have money and are always broke, you will be, too. Conversely, if you are surrounding yourself with wealthy, fulfilled, and successful people, you will end up being one of them, as well. My mentor once told me something I will NEVER forget: "Your net worth is determined by your network!" Choose your friends and associates wisely. So, which choices are you currently making towards your success?

CHAPTER SIX

Embrace Change or Die

"Find someone that loves your flaws, cause, and all."

- Boo and Moka

His name was Boo.
He was tall, dark-skinned, and had sexy lips and the prettiest brown eyes.

This was during a time when guys were trying to holla at me on a regular basis. I was about sixteen or seventeen years old, and I was *bad*. My skin was chocolate, my hair was thick, and my bow-legged legs were, too! After the experience with my last boyfriend, I would always shy away from those guys I really didn't know and grow up with, but Boo was able to get in where no one else could. We were from the same block. We grew up together, and we were always familiar with one another. We knew the same people.

I will never forget the night that Melle Mel let him used his car to drop me off at home one day. I always knew the "block" Boo, or in other words, the persona that he portrayed on the block. Confident, cool, and collected. I knew that outside version of Boo. But on that ride home, I discovered another side to this man. He began to talk, and I realized that he was actually very shy. That was a shock to me.

Boo was a heroin boy. He had more money, or paper, than any of the other dope boys at the time. He was in the most profitable part of the city making it happen. Standing over six feet tall, he had an intimidating stature, and he was running things. So, for me to find out that this man was really shy was unbelievable. It made me even become more intrigued by him. I felt like he exposed his heart to me. We exchanged phone numbers that night, and that was the beginning.

I had a homegirl named Candise, and we were thick as thieves. Candise was seeing Boo's homeboy, Bunny Rabbit. It was almost inevitable that with this undeniable attraction we felt, Boo and I were going to end up together. We all started kickin' it, and before I knew it, he was my boyfriend.

On my birthday, which is in February, Boo took me to the Chinese Restaurant. It was there that he gave me my very first pair of Jordans. It was freezing cold outside, and he also gave me *his* red, white and blue Tommy Hilfiger jacket off his own back! That was the moment I knew I loved this man. It's zero-degree weather, and this man is taking off his coat and putting it on me?! I had never experienced this kind of love before. I had never known a man to show his affection towards me and back it up financially, either. My nickname back then was Moka, from that point on, it was Boo and Moka. Moka and Boo. Point blank period!

I was so down for Boo that I would do anything for him. I was a rider. We used to call the police the "Jump Out Boys" back then. They would ride down the block, and one of the cops would be driving the car. As the car was still moving, the other cops would jump out the back and front seat and try to snatch up the dope boys to try to shake them down. When you could see them coming Boo would take all the money, anything incriminating that he might have had in his pockets, and he would give it to me to hold. When they were done shaking him down, he knew that when I gave it back to him, every dime and every gram would be accounted for. He didn't have to worry about any of it. I wasn't going to play him or, for that matter, let anyone else play him, either. He was my heart.

He was the first one to put heroin in my hands. Boo wasn't trying to get me started in the game nor did he condone it. I was already selling weed with the P.L.S. girls. It was more like, I was asking him for some money, and he said, "I ain't got it, but take this. Go make a couple of dollars." He had me sell 2 bags for $15, and it was the quickest thing to ever leave my hands. I went up to the top of the street, and it was sold that quickly! I knew I was on to something at that point. That money was just too easy (so it seemed). This wasn't something Boo approved of, as far as I got deep into selling it. He was just trying to look out for me that one time, because I had no money, but it really just opened me up to wanting more.

Once we really got used to selling all types of stuff, the P.L.S. girls had it made. We could travel and cross lines and territories with no problems. The guys were already making their money, so they didn't care about us coming through and doing our little thang. We could post up at Radios, which was a Mom & Pop corner store at the bottom of an apartment building, or we might hang around outside of B&B's, which was a black-owned restaurant. One of our favorite places to go to get business was The Trailer, which was an actual single-wide trailer in the middle of an empty parking lot that had been converted into what was basically a food truck. They stayed open until 3AM, and they sold the very best French fries, Polish boys, and chicken wings in the city.

Now, Boo had been seeing a girl – that we will call Renee – off and on around this time, as well. I was hearing rumors that he was still seeing this girl, and one day Renee says she is pregnant with Boo's child. Remember, we are all teenagers. No one really had any kids. So, when she said that she was pregnant, it was like, GAME OVER. Now he has a baby mama, and she's won I can't compete with that and I'm not trying to. For the rest of his life, like it or not, she is going to be in his life. I was devastated. It broke my heart to the core.

No matter what, I was still down for him. The thing was, even before we had slept together or became a couple, this was my homie. This was my *friend*, so I always had love for him. I was always going to be there for him, no matter what. We had history.

Then, Boo got caught up and eventually ended up going to jail. Around this time, he was supposed to be my date for the senior prom. I can remember one morning going to the county jail to visit him, being in the front of the line and then Renee walked in pregnant as ever. We were both there at the same time and then they called my name so I can go back to see him. When I finally got up there, he was acting different, funny, like he wasn't happy to see me. Here I was, thinking I was holding him down, coming to see him and riding for him, and his face was all frowned up.

"Man… she knows you're here. You know what I'm saying? Man, just go." He stressed.

"What?!" I knew he was talking about her. She was behind me in the line. Renee had been visiting him downtown at the county jail, just like me but this was the first time we came the same time and same day SMH.

"She knows you're here. Man, she's pregnant. I don't want any problems with her. Just go." I'd never seen that kind of distance in his eyes.

Damn, I thought.

I will never forget that.

That changed everything. I couldn't believe it. He had just chosen her over me.

Life went on. Boo did his bid, and when he got out of jail, he went to live with Renee. We stopped talking during that time. We would see each other in the neighborhood, but we weren't together any more.

#DisableYourLabels

Around this time, I really threw myself into the rap game. I was doing shows; I had my own apartment downtown. Getting into the music business allowed me to meet some of the biggest up and coming artists in the industry. It was a great opportunity that opened doors. I was a part of the 2nd Generation Ohio Players. We were like family: Big Heff, Finch, Trife, Mz. Fin, and Deyoz: we had the city on lock.

As the only female in the group, people couldn't believe my flow was so raw and so cold. I knew that I was able to flow this way because I was really living that life. I was able to take the life that I was living and translate it into the music. There wasn't another female, or even another guy, who could touch me! I wasn't making this stuff up; this was my life that I was rapping about. My home girls would come to my shows and support me.

During that time, we performed at the *Up in Smoke Tour*, opening up for Dr. Dre and Snoop Dogg. I was on the same mix tape with 50 Cent before he was *the* 50 Cent. We opened up for Lil Flip, Scarface, and any hot artist that would come through the city at that time. My rap name was Mz. Fin. Life was coming fast and strong.

In the midst of all of this, people I had grown up with were dying and going to jail all around me. It was getting really intense in Cleveland. I began to feel like I needed to get out now or I might not make it out at all. I didn't think I would live to see the age of eighteen, and so when I did, I wanted to make sure that I would make it to see the age of twenty-one.

I felt like I was in between a rock and a hard place. On one hand, I was giving my home girls a form of escape. The hood was excited to know someone who was doing something different with their life. My shows gave them a reason to dress up and get out. Most people didn't really venture out of the hood. We all felt like nothing but problems came from traveling outside of the norm. Deep down, I even believed that the rape I experienced at age sixteen was because I had dared to explore life outside of our neighborhood. So, being able to get fly, get your hair and nails done, and go see one of your home girls on stage at a real live show was unheard of.

Now, I had to decide. Do I stay and risk facing the same fate so many of my homies had already faced, just to be the example for others? Or should I answer the call that I felt was beckoning me to leave Cleveland? I felt like it was now or never, and I didn't want to stay there in the small pond and drown.

My aunt, Danielle, was living in Atlanta, and she called me one day to say that she was leaving her kids father. This was my favorite aunt. Remember that my mother was the oldest of ten children. Danielle was the youngest, and after her, I was the first grandchild born. So, of everyone in the family, we were the youngest, even though she must have been ten or twelve years older than me. She was the only one who would come to check up on me when I was living with my great aunt, Aunt Shirley. Aunt Danielle would come pick me up and take me to many places. In fact, she took me to see my very first concert! We went to see Kriss Kross perform, and I'll never forget it.

So, I was already thinking about wanting to leave Cleveland, and Aunt Danielle called. She said that she needed help with her three small kids since she was leaving her boyfriend, and she asked if I wanted to come down to help her out since she was going to be on her own. I got excited. I felt like I was stagnant in Ohio, and that I could do so much more in Atlanta. I thought that I would be able to pursue my music career and just do so much more.

I decided to leave my place, my current live-in boyfriend, Meel, and everything that I had ever known behind to chase my dreams in the "A".

DISABLE YOUR LABELS
Never be afraid of change

Other than taxes and death, change is the only other thing guaranteed in life; so, don't be afraid to take chances in life, in love, and on your dreams. Some will be hits, and some will be misses. I know people that have never left the city they were born in, so they couldn't tell you what another state even looked like. Disable the label that you have to stay in a certain city, set, state, relationship, area or even job for that matter. The one thing we were all given freely at birth was the power of choice. Never be afraid to choose a different direction for your life. Never be afraid to follow your dreams no matter who approves or dislikes your decisions.

In order to elevate in life, you're going to have to change one of three things or all three. People, places, or things. What do I mean by that? You have got to change the people you are around. It doesn't matter if they are close to you or if they get offended or not. Even in the Bible, God told Abraham to get away from around his family, friends, but don't worry "I'm going to take care of you. I'm going to bless the people that bless you, but I'm also going to curse that people that curse you. "

Gen 12:1-3 "¹Now the Lord had said unto Abram, Get thee out of thy country, and from thy kindred, and from thy father's house, unto a land that I will show thee: ² And I will make of thee a great nation, and I will bless thee, and make thy name great; and thou shalt be a blessing: ³ And I will bless them that bless thee, and curse him that curseth thee: and in thee shall all families of the earth be blessed."

So, this is a 3-step process God is giving us to be blessed and embrace change. 1. "Get away from your comfort zone", get away from the people you call friends, family because they are actually holding you back. Understand, everything will work out, you're too comfortable around them and you won't step out on faith. (Remember the GPS destination we talked about earlier as long as you have the destination, you will get there.) 2. "Go where I am telling you to go", or in other words do what I am telling you to do. This is where a lot of people miss the mark because if they can't touch it, feel it, smell it, or see it they don't believe it's real. You have to believe it, then, you'll see it: not see it, then believe it. Let's be honest, do you think Steve Jobs (the creator of the Apple) saw the iPhone in his hand first before he created it?? No, he had a vision a destination for it first, then, came the physical manifestation of it. Why do we feel or look at things any differently? We need to have the vision/destination first "write the vision and make it plan." and then i promise the manifestation of it will come if you don't give up. Finally, 3. "Then I will bless you! " I want you to understand there are blessings in obedience, there are blessings in being disciplined, there are blessings in having structure and order. Even the Bible says in 1 Corinthians 14:40, "Let all things be done decently and in order." A lot of times when we aren't achieving our goals or visions in life, it's because we are out of order in some way or doing something that we aren't supposed to be doing. The end of the verse says, "I will bless them that bless you and curse them that curse you, and all the families in the earth will be blessed by you." I know what you're thinking how is this possible. What does this mean?

A lot of times, we can be worried about the wrong things when change takes place, or when we are asked to change. We worry about failing, failure, haters, others opinions and views of us. That's why He says I will bless the people that bless you, so don't worry about that, but I will also curse the people that curse you. So, God is telling you, don't worry about your haters, don't worry about your enemy, because I'm going to take care of them, I got you. Why is that? Why does God care about your future, your prosperity, your business, or even your life for that matter? Because verse 3 says, "in you all the families of the earth will be blessed." Let me give you some examples. When Apple was created, who was blessed by the iPhone, iPad, Mac? Just Steve Job's family, friends, neighbors? No, it was the entire world blessed by these products "all the families in the earth was blessed by it." Which also resulted in changing the way we communicate and we will never be the same again because of it. Now you can fight the change and say you don't want to use a cellphone, try to use a Pigeon or Dove to deliver a message: people will look at you like your crazy..lol. Nowadays, it's easier for all the families in the earth to be blessed by you, because of the internet, things can go viral, you can sell products and services internationally. The word 'viral', the word 'international', the word 'World Wide Web', the word 'internet' means "all the families in the earth can be blessed by you!"

The Seven Responses to Change
Myles Munroe

1. You Can Resist Change
2. You Can Ignore Change
3. You Can Accept Change
4. You Can Adjust to Change
5. You Can Manage Change
6. You Can Become A Victim of Change

7. YOU CAN PREPARE AND PLAN FOR CHANGE

Most people think they can avoid, resist, or ignore change as if they have a choice. Guess what? That only hurts you. For example, when Apple came out with iPod, it allowed you to access 5000 songs in the palm of your hand. So, for everyone that was stuck on a CD collection or tape collection or even DVD, they were left in the dust. You can barely find a place to sell you a CD now and there is only one small section at Walmart that sells DVD now. In other words, whether you like change or not, whether you're ready for change or not, it's going to happen. My advice is to prepare for change. This is what I was never told, or what I never understood growing up. If I'm sixteen, how can I prepare for when I turn eighteen, or when I turn twenty-one to get out of my parents' house? Begin to prepare and plan for the change so you can have more control over it, then trying to avoid it. If you fail to plan, then you plan to fail. Take the limits off yourself: take the limits off God. But, change is the only way to achieve that success you are designed for. So, embrace change reject doubt and begin to live the life you deserve.

CHAPTER SEVEN

Trust the Process

"I have not failed. I've just found 10,000 ways that won't work."

- Thomas Edison

Historically Black Colleges and Universities (HBCUs), and I didn't have the money for the spot on the tour. My cousin told me that one of the girls had paid for her ticket, and for whatever reasons, she now couldn't go. I was bold enough to slip right into the group, counting on the fact that no one would catch on, and for the whole tour, everyone was calling me by her name! When opportunity knocks, open the door. Our tour included Alabama A&M, Clark Atlanta University, Spelman College, and Florida A&M.

Once we got to Atlanta, I was amazed. I had never seen a city filled with so many educated and upwardly-mobile Black people! The vibe was just so different there, and I was in awe that places like this really existed. It was such a stark contrast from what I was used to in Cleveland. From then on, Atlanta would be all I would think about when I envisioned my own future.

When I finally made it there as an adult, however, it wasn't anything like what I thought. To my dismay, my aunt hadn't left her kids father, after all. Instead, I found myself living in a small hotel room with her, her man, and three small children! I was frustrated and started to feel like I had made the wrong choice (even though I loved them babies to death.) I expressed my frustration to Meel, who was still my boyfriend at the time, and he told me to calm down. He said that he had an uncle who lived in Atlanta, and he would come out to be with me soon enough.

Before I had left Atlanta, Meel and I had been living together. Meel was several years older than me. He would post up on South Boulevard, which was known as the crack block. Meel was also the weed man, too. We had always been cool years before our relationship. When Boo went to jail, Meel was the one who ended up taking me to prom. He was also the one who would school me to the game. He was the first to really teach me about weight (or weighing the drugs before selling it). Meel's big brother was an O.G., and he would school Meel, who would pass the information down to me. We had started out as friends, but after the scene at the jail with Boo happened, it became something more. I would often express my dreams of leaving the city with Meel. He didn't want to see me leave, but he always understood my reasons for wanting to go.

I found myself in a predicament. I swore to myself that when I went to Atlanta, I wasn't going to sell drugs anymore and I refused to strip to make money, even though I could have easily done either one. I had moved there to do bigger things. I kept thinking that I just needed to make enough money for me to get my own room somewhere instead of living with my aunt and her family. Then, I found out about something that they called "Bitch Boxing."

Boxing was a quick way to make money without having to do anything illegal. It was held in the strip club. In between the dancers dancing, two girls would strap on the gloves, and the club would erect a boxing rink right on stage. We were the entertainment in between the entertainment.

Two women would go three rounds, and the men would throw tips on the stage that the two women would later split. If your breast fell out of your top while you were boxing, that would mean more tips. The better your outfit, the better money you'd get. If you did a bomb combo and knocked the other girl out, there came even more tips. The more blood, the more tips!

Now, my grandfather and my father used to box when they were younger, so I came from a line of fighters. Here I am, coming from a place where I used to fight for free, and in my first night Boxing, I cleared about $200 easy. I didn't have to risk going to jail or shaking my butt to do it. I knew I had found my niche. This went on for a few months, but eventually, I realized that it just wasn't going to work for me in Atlanta. I decided to go back home.

I went back to Cleveland, and I was off and on again with Meel. On July 11, 2001, exactly twenty years after my own father's death to the day, I began to have excruciating pain in my belly. I had no idea what was happening. I have an extremely high tolerance for pain, but this was unlike anything I'd ever felt before. I thought I was dying. My best friend, Markita, who was Candise's older sister, came and got me to take me to the hospital.

The doctor said that I had an ectopic pregnancy or a pregnancy that had occurred in my fallopian tubes, and not in my uterus. I had miscarried the fetus. It was very early in my pregnancy, and Meel and I had no idea that I was even pregnant. The doctor performed a laparoscopy, finding that the fallopian tube had been damaged and needed to be removed. He warned that I would probably never be able to have children, and the chances that I would ever have a healthy pregnancy were very low. I was devastated. The whole experience was so traumatic that I have blocked out a lot of what happened during that time to protect myself. A lot of people who experience miscarriages go through the same sort of thing, blocking out parts that are too painful to remember.

Some may think that it seems superstitious for me to think this way, but I felt that the whole thing happened for a reason. I know one thing for sure, and that is that God doesn't make any mistakes. My miscarriage happened literally twenty years after my father's murder, which happened on July 11, 1981. I couldn't help but feel that was a sign that kids were not the plan God had for my life, at least at that moment.

After the miscarriage, I decided that I would give Atlanta another chance. I needed to leave Cleveland behind me for good. I moved back out, and this time I had a different mentality. I decided I would go legit, and I would work my way through it. Meel ended up coming out to Atlanta with me and linking up with his uncle. I threw myself into my work.

I would work back to back shifts as a waitress. I'd work my Waffle house graveyard shift from 11PM to 7AM, serving everyone who had the late-night munchies and leaving the clubs. Then I'd go home and rest a minute, and the next thing I know, I'd be headed to my Longhorn Steakhouse shift, serving lunch and dinner from 10AM to 6PM. I eventually got a job waitressing at TGI Fridays, too.

Sometimes, your plan for your own life may be one thing, but all too often, life has another thing planned for you. Or maybe you have no plan at all, and so it feels like you are just going wherever the wind may take you. I always encourage planning, because if you fail to plan, then you plan to fail.

DISABLE YOUR LABELS

Is the glass half empty or half full? – It is all about YOUR perception

I want you to disable your labels on perception and understand that things work out for your greater good. Even the Bible says in Romans 8:28, "And we know that *all things work together for good* to them that love God, to them who are the called according to his purpose." What I have learned is that it is not just the final destination that you should focus on, because in fact, it is usually the *journey* that will teach you what you need to know along the way. If you can appreciate the journey, then, when you do finally get to your destination, whatever that may be, it will be all that more satisfying to know you made it through all of the trials and tribulations for a reason.

I had no idea that my experiences selling drugs as a teenager would teach me how to formulate a crew around me that would support a common goal. It would also teach me sales - when it was time to re-up, that taught me how to order inventory. When everyone sold the same thing as you, we learned to cut deals 2 for $15 (sales and marketing), be creative. We knew all the smokers by name; so, they would rock with us and continue to come back to us over others that sold the exact same product (great customer service). When obstacles got in your way: police, robbers, haters etc. you learned to move a lot smoother, wiser, with purpose, waste no time, trust no one, and never take anything for granted (unstoppable work ethic). I didn't know that the rap shows I performed in Cleveland and other states would prepare me to speak in front of large crowds of people. Who would have thought that Boxing would make me have a thick skin. Allow me to be tough when faced with making rough decisions and facing people who wished me no good and remain sexy the whole time while going through it? How could I have known that having a painful miscarriage would make me appreciate the birth of my three beautiful children more than I would have ever known? The jobs I worked in Atlanta during those days taught me to have a positive work ethic, to never be afraid of hard work, hustle like there's no tomorrow and to outwork the next person to make it. It also taught me how rewarding it was to meet my own personal goals.

All of these things had to happen in order to make me the person that I am today. All of the experiences that you are going through right now, no matter whether they are good or bad, are also working towards your greater good. Believe it or not, without these things happening in your life, you will not be able to make it to your final destination. I connect with people all over the world; many are suicidal or ready to make a permanent decision over a temporary situation. Suicide should NEVER BE AN OPTION. Because the situation, problem, or challenge actually comes to promote you not demote you. If you can just understand the journey you go through along the way, is preparing you for something greater and the trial is there to help build you up and not tear you down, I believe you would look at trials a lot differently. Even the Bible says, to everything there is a season.

Ecclesiastes 3:1-8 (KJV)

[1] To every thing there is a season, and a time to every purpose under the heaven:

[2] A time to be born, and a time to die; a time to plant, and a time to pluck up that which is planted;

[3] A time to kill, and a time to heal; a time to break down, and a time to build up;

[4] A time to weep, and a time to laugh; a time to mourn, and a time to dance;

[5] A time to cast away stones, and a time to gather stones together; a time to embrace, and a time to refrain from embracing;

[6] A time to get, and a time to lose; a time to keep, and a time to cast away;

[7] A time to rend, and a time to sew; a time to keep silence, and a time to speak;

[8] A time to love, and a time to hate; a time of war, and a time of peace.

What does this mean? We are going to have good days, we are going to have bad days, we are going to have happy days, we are going to have sad days; it's all a part of the human experience. Psalm 30:5 says "For his anger endureth but a moment; in his favour is life: weeping may endure for a night, but joy cometh in the morning." In other words, we have to have balance, we have to have day and night, we have to have spring and fall, we have to have summer and winter. Let's be honest for those of us who leave in hot climates of extreme heat, we thank God it's not 110-degree Vegas summer all 365 days! For those of us in extreme cold climates like Canada where it can get to be like -20 degrees thank God winter don't last 365 days! Without hot summers you really don't have an appreciation for fall or winter, without extremely cold winters you don't have an appreciation for warm springs or summer. Again, without bad days, you really don't have an appreciation for good days. This is why I say the seasons or days, or pain, sorrow, challenge, or lack is all in preparation to turn into a season of joy, happiness, fulfillment, abundance, and prosperity but only if you continue moving forward. Don't get stuck in the situation, you are to go through the situation not stand there weeping in it.

My motto is this: "If you ask the right questions, then you'll get the right answers". Most people will ask the question "Why me?" To be honest, that is a horrible question to ask. Ask this: How can I overcome this situation even though I don't see a way out? Another example: How can I pass this graduate even though I failed last quarter, semester, or period (whatever it may be called)? The key is to not allow the situation to move you back, but how can you still move forward regardless of whatever challenge has presented itself.

If you have a glass of water in a cup that is filled about halfway, would you say that the glass is half way full, or would you say the glass is half way empty? It's all about how you look at things. You are on your own personal journey right now, and everyone must go through their own, in their own way. Trust the process and use these things to propel you forward. Learn from your life and use each part of your own adventure to create the person that you ultimately wish to be.

CHAPTER EIGHT

Speak Life

"... calleth those things that be not as though they were."

- Romans 4:17, KJV

I lived in Atlanta for a couple of years with Meel after the miscarriage. I worked at several waitressing jobs, and finally found my calling in sales. I began working at Dollar Thrifty Car Rental. I had always heard about how my mother broke records in the car rental business. My mother was known for being a hustler and being able to sell anything, and my father had the gift of gab. So, as their child, I was a natural born hustler with a serious mouthpiece who could sell a cup of water to the ocean.

I began having a lot of success in the sales industry. Meel and I broke up for good a year later, and in 2003, I decided to make a trip back home to Cleveland to visit. This was the first time I would be seeing Boo in about three or four years. He had grown another three inches, and he wasn't long and lanky anymore. Instead, he was buff and bald-headed, and he had my nose wide open once again. He wasn't seeing Renee anymore.

We reconnected, and he came out to visit me in Atlanta. It was great for me to show him my new environment. Boo loved it. He said the same thing that I did when I had first visited during that college tour that I took five years prior. This city was so different from Cleveland. I was living alone, but a year later, we were living together.

It felt like God was giving us a new start. I felt like things were finally happening for me the way that they were supposed to. In June of 2005, Boo and I bought a house, bought a truck and finally got married. In September of that same year, despite what I had been told by the doctors after my miscarriage that I would never have kids. We found out that I was pregnant. After I nervously let him know that I was expecting, Boo smiled a big cheesy grin and said, "Man, I been trying to get you pregnant for years!"

One day, I was sitting on the edge of my bed, peering out of the window and rubbing my pregnant belly. I was still in disbelief that I was really having my first child with a man that I loved more than anything. The phone ringing disrupted me from my daydream.

#DisableYourLabels

"Hello, Mrs. Sowell, this is your doctor's office. We have the results of your recent blood test. Do you have a moment to discuss them?" An unfamiliar lady's voice inquired on the other line.

"Sure..." A feeling of foreboding began to creep up the back of my neck.

"Ma'am, are you sitting down?"

"Yes," I hesitated. "What's up?"

As the nurse droned on and on about irregular results, she used terms I had never heard of before. A lot of the medical jargon went over my head, but I heard her say that my unborn child had a 50% chance of being born with Down's syndrome, and that even if he wasn't born with that, he'd have a 75% chance of having Spina Bifida.

"Ma'am!" I interrupted her. "Ma'am! You are going to have to slow down, and you're going to need to speak *English*! What is Spina Bifida?!"

"To be brief, Spina Bifida is a birth defect in which a baby's spinal cord fails to develop properly. This defect cannot be cured, and it will affect the baby's ability to walk properly, could cause neurological difficulties, and may cause incontinence and the inability to control his or her bowels."

I was speechless. Hearing my shocked silence, she said softly, "Mrs. Sowell, I understand that this is a very sensitive subject, but the doctor suggested, you may want to consider an abortion."

"WHAT?!" I screamed out, clutching my belly as desperately as I was clutching the phone. My voice echoed through the house. I stared out of the window at the perfect trees in our backyard and suddenly felt like I was outside of myself as if I was having an out of body experience.

As a woman, one of the things that you assume should come naturally to you is to be able to become a mother. I suddenly felt like less than a woman. Here I was, my nose spreading, my hair flowing long and thick, and my belly looking round and healthy, and this woman had somehow destroyed it all with one single phone call.

"... not everyone can handle having a child with... may want to consider all of your options... speak to Mr. Sowell..." The nurse continued on in an even, unemotional tone. I literally at that point was only catching every other word that came from her mouth.

God, why me? I screamed out in my own mind. I felt my hands shaking, knocking the phone receiver against my ear over and over again. The walls of the house began to close in on me. *Why are you doing this to me? I did everything right. I got married first. I bought a house. We have the big truck. I have everything I need to take good care of this baby!*

I must've cried out and dropped the phone, because the next thing I remember is Boo rushing into the room. He was holding me close to him and trying to calm me down. I felt the hot tears running down my face as I looked at his mouth and saw his lips moving, but I don't recall the exact words that were coming from them. Inexplicably, I was able to attempt to communicate what she had said to me.

"Aw, c'mon, that ain't gonna happen. Trust me. And *even* if it did, we would still love him. That's my son. Don't worry." Boo consoled me.

Easy for you to say, I thought. *You already have other healthy kids! This is my first.* I really felt miserable, because all of his children with other women were healthy and fine. That meant to me that I was the one who was responsible for this! I was the one who was broken. Something was wrong with me. I'm now zero for two! And I am his wife. Not this man's girlfriend or his side piece. I was this man's wife, and I couldn't give him a healthy baby boy?

"Look, first of all, didn't they say that you would never have kids after your miscarriage? Now look, you're pregnant. Second, no matter what, we will love him just the same because he is our son. Third, we are not having any abortion, no matter what these people say. No son of mine will be born with any defect, anyway." Boo repeated.

You may have heard someone use the term, "Speak things into existence."

I had heard the term but until that moment never really understood what it really meant. It means that life and death are in the power of your tongue, and whatever seeds you sow with your words are the fruit that you will end up producing. Therefore, if you don't enjoy the fruit that you are seeing, sow different seeds! An apple seed will never produce oranges. You *must* speak life, speak love, and speak into existence the outcome that you want to happen.

At that time, we had to make one of the most important decisions of our lives. We made the decision to keep our baby no matter what the doctors said or thought. Next, we made a conscious choice to speak life over our baby constantly. Just like the old folks would say, prepare for the worst but hope for the best.

Not only did my blood test warn that our baby might have a high risk of Down's syndrome or Spina Bifida, but the doctors let me know that I had a rare blood type, as well. I had an O negative blood type, which could complicate matters further. They gave me what they called the Rhogam injection, which would help me not develop antibodies that would attack not only the baby inside of me but any subsequent children I would ever have. It would seem, to anyone else that the odds were stacked against us.

Since we are humans, we inevitably experienced pain, doubt and fear, but we knew that we had made a final decision and stood behind it with all we had. We spoke words over our situation that matched the results that we expected. This was one of the hardest things I have ever had to do – ignore the doctor's warnings and step out in faith. This was also the first time I learned about the power of affirmations.

Affirmations are the verbal actions or processes of affirming something or being affirmed. My great aunt, Buttercup, was the one who would call it speaking life over your situation. Either way, it's a verbal declaration of what you want. Small-minded people might call it lying. In the hood, we sometimes referred to it as "fake it 'til you make it." Whichever way you'd like to look at it, please understand that your words will make or break you.

"I will have a quick and easy delivery of a healthy baby boy."

That was my daily affirmation in 2006. I probably repeated this to myself at least one hundred times a day! I made sure that I said it ten times over again, and always at ten different times during the day. I'd say it when I woke up in the morning, while I was in the shower getting ready for my day, while I was cooking, on my way to work, on my way home from work, before I went to sleep at night – you name it!

Before I knew it, I had developed the habit of speaking this affirmation on a regular basis. Something even more miraculous was that I eventually began to really *believe* this to be true. I was slowly coming to believe that I would actually have a healthy baby boy during a quick and easy delivery, despite the doctors telling me that I wouldn't and *shouldn't*.

During my pregnancy, well-meaning women would share their pregnancy stories with me. They'd talk about their child birth experiences, and they'd tell me how it took them two whole days or thirty-six hours to have their baby. I would immediately thank them for sharing their story, then I would say, "But that won't be me. I will have a quick and easy delivery of a healthy baby boy," and walk away.

It may seem funny, but I would get away from them as soon as I could before they had an opportunity to plant a negative seed in my mind. I had enough battles to deal with without taking on new things to think about. You must watch what you allow people to say around you or to you, because people subconsciously want their bad experience to become your bad experience. My grandma used to say,

#DisableYourLabels

"Beware of the dog that carries the bone, because the dog which brings you a bone will also take one." In other words, watch a person who always has something to tell you, because they may not have your best interest in mind.

I remember very clearly waking up on May 3, 2006, five days before what would've been my father's birthday. I felt like I needed to use the bathroom. No matter how many times I tried, nothing happened. There was so much intense pain in my lower belly, but I still didn't think that I was going into labor. It was my first child, and from what I had seen on television, the lady's water always broke first before they rushed her off to the hospital. I didn't see any water, so I didn't understand what was going on.

I phoned my mother, and sure enough, she told me that I was probably having my baby! It seemed like as soon as she said that – BAM! – a contraction hit me like a bolt of lightning. I started feeling waves of pain throughout my whole body like I had never felt before. I thought to myself, *you gotta be kidding me.*

The waves of pain started coming quicker and quicker, with each new one growing stronger than the last. Then it felt like a relay race. The first waves were ten minutes apart, giving me a little time to rest in between. Soon it was eight minutes, and then every five minutes I was doubled over. I prayed to the Lord to help me as Boo drove me to the hospital.

Now I understood why women on television were always screaming so loud when they were in labor. I used to think that they were just playing it up. *It can't be all that bad!* I thought. I was absolutely right. It wasn't that bad. IT WAS WAY WORSE! The most important thing that I could do was to try and breathe and concentrate on having a healthy baby boy. That might sound easy but trying to remember to breathe through your contractions is very hard to do when they are coming harder and faster each time. Panicking only makes it worse. Screaming, cussing, and fussing just intensify your struggle.

And then, just like that, I was a mother. After only six hours of labor, I held in my arms the most beautiful thing I had ever seen. Yes, I had a quick and easy delivery of a healthy baby boy, just as I had affirmed.

There may be something that you are going through right now. It may seem like your trials are coming stronger and faster each day. I am telling you to concentrate on getting through it. Breathe. Focus on the end result that you want to achieve. The same rules and basic principles that I had to follow to get through my childbirth still apply. Affirm and believe in your desired result no matter what the situation looks like. No matter what anyone tries to say or speak over you – *believe!*

Look, I didn't know what I was really doing with these affirmations, but what I didn't know then, I know now. As I have said earlier in this book, there is always a formula. There is a formula for turning impossible into I'M POSSIBLE. I would love to share this process with you. If you are currently going through something that seems impossible, or if you feel like no one could possibly understand or relate, let me share this with you.

I can't tell you about anything that I know nothing about. I can only share with you what I know first-hand and what the experience taught me. I want to show you step by step what I did to overcome a situation that could have very well cost my son his life. Even if your situation may not be as dramatic as mine was, you have to treat it like life or death, because depending on what you're going through, it just might be.

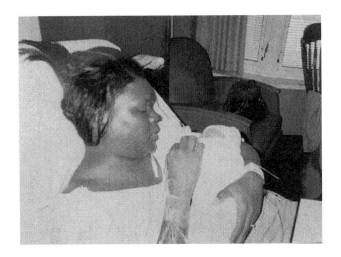

DISABLE YOUR LABELS
Turning Impossible into I'M POSSIBLE

- *Decide* – You can't flip flop back and forth. You cannot be unstable. Make a real decision and run with it. There is no looking back, wondering, "What if...?" There is only one outcome, as far as you're concerned.

- *Speak Life* – Once you have made the final decision, speak life over that decision daily and hourly if you have to. Remember, your decision is a seed, and your words are like water and sunshine to that seed; the more water and sun you give it, the more it will grow. The more you speak life, the more it feels like reality.

- *Get One Person to Agree with You* – Even Jesus said *"If two of you shall agree on earth as touching anything that they shall ask, it shall be done for them of my Father which is in heaven."* Boo was able to hold me accountable on the days that I didn't have the strength to speak life over my son. You need at least one person to believe with you. I don't care if you must start a support group on Facebook, IG, or Snapchat just get someone to support and agree with you.
- *Protect Your Space* – You must consciously stay away from negative people. Some people don't even realize that they're being negative. Their intentions might be good. But when you know that you have seed in the ground, you must be sure it is planted in the right type of soil. Weeds will grow and choke your seed out if you are not careful. When you hear people starting to speak negatively, stay away! Even if they are "joking". Don't stand for it; remove those negative thoughts because it's like pulling the weeds up from your garden.
- *Affirm Your Desired Result* – Every day, you must water your seed with both your words and your actions. You will either attract or distract a certain type of result depending on what you do or say. Don't make the mistake of sabotaging your own self!
- *Establish a Timeframe and Deadline* – What is the time frame that it will take for you to reach your desired goal? It's

not good enough to say, "One day I will…" or "Someday, I'm going to…" I'll tell you a secret. There is no such day of the week as *some day or one day (trust me I've checked every calendar)*. So, just like the calendar is specific, so must you be. As in, "This will get done on Tuesday, October 13th, 2020." You need to be just that specific. It may not happen exactly on that date. As a matter of fact, it may happen two weeks before that date! But by being specific, you are letting the Universe know that this is what you want, and you are serious about it.

Am I perfect? NO!! What I am is a woman who has found a way to disable the labels that others have put on me and in return achieve MY DESIRE RESULTS. It doesn't matter what label someone or something has put on you! Mother, father, brother, sister, grandmother, grandfather, teacher, friends, society, etc. You are more than a conqueror! Disable the labels others have placed on you: tall, skinny, short, fat, ugly, broke, ghetto, red neck, stupid, broke, poor, nerd, felon, single mother, divorced, black, white, uneducated, etc. Take the labels off of your life, and replace them with words that speak life, love, and liberty over you. You are intelligent, pretty, wealthy, smart, and can overcome any situation you face.

I didn't even know back then that I was creating a formula, or following one, for that matter. I just know that this is what I did. When I was pregnant with my son, it was the first time that I had ever tried this, but it wouldn't be the last. It has worked for me every single time.

So, what are you going through right now? Is someone telling you that you cannot achieve something? Is that someone YOU? It is time to stop allowing your situation to rule you. Apply this simple formula and move away from fear, doubt, and unbelief. It is time to start putting your words and actions into motion and get some things done for you!

CHAPTER NINE

On a Mission to Commission

"Look in the mirror... That's your competition."

- Author Unknown

I was helping my grandad put up groceries once when I was about six years old. He looked down at me and said, "Grandbaby," My granddad could never remember my name. "When you grow up, make sure you get a good job with benefits, a pension, and a 401k plan. Preferably, get a job with the state or in corporate America in your early twenties. That way, by the time you're fifty-five, you can retire and live out your golden years stress free."

"Wow, Granddaddy, that's a long time to be working at one job, isn't it?" In my young confused mind, I was trying to understand what he had just said while trying not to drop the eggs.

"Well," he said as he continued to put the groceries away, "It's called job security. You want to get you a job where you know you can be secure and retired, like me."

"Ok." I said, as I folded up the last brown paper bag.

Almost fifteen years later, I would give old Granddad's advice a shot. I can remember showing up to the Dollar Thrifty Car Rental building in Atlanta with my navy-blue slacks and plain, white, button-down shirt for my first day in corporate America. Now, I was raised on cornbread and collard greens, so my pants fit way different from all the other females in the office.

"Who's the new girl with the big butt?" They whispered, as if I couldn't hear them.

I didn't let their twisted lips and rolling eyes affect me. I wasn't there to make friends; I was there to make money! As time progressed, I threw myself into being a top salesperson. It wasn't hard. I have always felt that a drug dealer is nothing more than a salesman at their core. If you can go through all of stress and unpredictability of selling illegal drugs and be successful in that dark environment, selling something legally without the risk of death or jail looming over your head is a piece of cake! One thing that I do know for sure is that a dope man's hustle is unlike anyone else's.

#DisableYourLabels

I would liken it to learning how to swim. Someone who has been raised in upper middle-class America gets slowly accustomed to becoming a salesperson. They may take a few courses in college and listen to some motivational self-help audiobooks on their way to their part-time job at the mall. Eventually, they find a sales or marketing job, and they apply their knowledge to the job to be successful – like a small child slowly being introduced to the water.

Me? I learned how to swim by drowning. I started life in the nine-foot end of the pool. This is why I stand firmly behind the belief that drug dealers can make the best salespeople and entrepreneurs. The other people in the office were selling for a living. I had been selling to stay alive and survive! I wasn't frightened by rejection, which is why most people are turned off about trying to sell in corporate America. I was used to hustling and not taking no for an answer.

Once I started working in the car rental industry, it didn't take me very long before I was number ten in sales in the entire region. At twenty-one years old, I quickly moved my way up to being the number one sales agent in less than two years and the youngest person to ever hit those ranks in My Fortune 500 Company. By the time I worked my second corporate job, not only was I number one, I also became the first African-American woman to do so.

After learning how to master fighting for my freedom in the streets and always watching my back in the hood, nobody in corporate America could catch me. I was taking over six hundred customers a month, doubling everyone else's numbers. This just excited me even more to see how well I could do. Other co-workers had a bad habit of watching me and worrying about how I could possibly be doing what they could never do. One thing I know is that the winners of a race aren't the ones turning their heads from side to side watching the other competitors. The ones who win are facing straight forward, and they are concerned with nothing else but the finish line. My only competition is myself.

The long days, and sometimes nights, didn't faze me. I figured, if I can make decent money and not have to worry about being robbed, going to jail, or having the police kick down my door, what did I care about working late? I loved the peace of mind that a real nine-to-five (sometimes six or seven) job offered me.

I would often open and close the store in the same day. I started training other employees for free. When others would call off work, I would work outside in the rain just to show that I was a team player. The managers had begun to rely on me for everything. When the numbers were low, call Desirae. If a manager needed to go on break, call Desirae. If they needed coverage for absent employees, call Desirae.

That was all fine by me, because I was making money hand over fist, and to this day I know that I have made over four or five million dollars in commission sales in corporate America. I could never settle for another hourly job, because I was worth way more than even fifteen or twenty dollars an hour. In my biggest sales month, I have made over seven thousand dollars at twenty five years old.

I have since worked several different commission sales jobs. I have always been a top performer, if not *the* top performer in my position. Why is that? What makes me so special? What makes me different? Some people will see my success and want to try to copy my exact sales pitch. They figure that there must be a magical set of words and a certain way that I say them that makes me sell more than anyone else. Others will ask me what books I have read. What training have I taken? Who is my mentor? Who is my business consultant?

While all of those things are important to the progression of a great salesperson, that is not the reason why I stand out. I could sit here and tell you everything that I know about opening your pitch, assuming the sale, collecting yeses, and perfecting the close. I can give you sales techniques, like letting the customer know what is in it for them, creating value, and asking open-ended questions. I could tell you *all* of this, and you may still never make one sale.

What I *cannot* teach you is how to be HUNGRY. One thing that I *always* had was hunger. When I was back at home in Cleveland, selling drugs, I was hungry. I needed to make those sales. I needed to *eat!* I transferred that hunger to Atlanta and corporate America. You must want it more than you want anything else. You *must* know how to go hard or go home. I have seen people who were perfectly capable of selling choose a $12-an-hour customer service job over a sales position that could possible paid over six figures, because it was strictly commission. Now, why would anyone ever do that? I will tell you why – FEAR. (False Evidence Appearing Real) Your hunger *must* outweigh your fear. If it doesn't, then nothing anyone says to you will ever matter.

Even if you never plan on selling anything in your life, you need to apply this same principle to everything else you desire from life. Your hunger for that thing must outweigh your fear of failure at all times. What do you hunger for? Is it your goals to graduate school or be the first in your family to complete school? Do you hunger for a healthy relationship with your parents, friends, or loved ones? Do you hunger for a stable house, a place to call home, and foundation for your future? Do you desire the ability to raise your children to be happy and healthy in a positive environment? Just how much do you want it? What will you do to achieve it? Is your hunger strong enough to beat out any fear that you may have? If it is, then trust me, *nothing* can keep you from your goals!

DISABLE YOUR LABELS

How can you expect a return and you're not
willing to invest?

Money is an area that will make or break your family, a
marriage lack of money has your parents divorcing. Money is
an area that can cost you your house, your car, your college
choices. Listen, money is an area that can cost you your life!
You know how many people have gone to jail over money,
been hospitalized over money, even died over money! These
are some of the labels we must disable: "We can't afford it! I
will never have enough money. I'm robbing Peter to pay Paul
as my grandmother would say. Or I'm broke as a joke, or
money doesn't grow on trees." All the jargon we speak over
our finances will attract or distract us from the goal we
actually want to achieve or receive. Know what you want to
make and stop settling until you make it! Point Blank Period!
There is no law that says everyone else in the world can make
the amount they want to make and live their dream life, but
you can't. For a while, I used to feel that way until I realized I
had to make it happen because no one else will, and in
actuality it's not anyone else's job to make sure my dreams

come true. You can blame your teacher, principle, parents, job, spouse, kids, childhood, your environment, your past or present situation. But if we're being real, what is the common denominator in any of these situations? YOU ARE. Disable the label that, you are not good enough, you are not smart enough, you are not worthy of abundance etc. because truth is, you are, my love. You have to own the life you want to live; you have to own the life you want your children to live and don't let anything stop you. Even the Bible says in Psalm 37:4, "Delight thyself also in the Lord: and he shall give thee the desires of thine heart." It is God will to give us the desires of our heart. It also says in 3 John 1:2 NIV: "Beloved, I wish above all things that thou mayest prosper and be in health, even as thy soul prosperth." YES THE BIBLE SAYS GOD WANTS YOU TO PROSPER!

Your WHY must be strong enough to outweigh your fears. In other words, the reason why you want to achieve your goals has to be so strong till you won't let the word 'no' or any other obstacles get in your way. When you look at money, I want you to understand first and foremost it's only numbers. Let me say that again, it's only numbers. So, what you really have to master is the numbers game. Remember I said I would double the customer everyone else would take because my numbers showed in order to reach my goal financially, I needed 10 sales per day in one category and 5 sales each day in another category, and in order to make those sales in each category I needed a minimum of 50 customers a day. While everyone else would complain when they took 20-25 customers in a day, I was hungry for a minimum of 50; clearly, we didn't have the same goals or the same 'why.

Make sure you have a game plan; no coach just heads out on the field without knowing who the quarterback, offense or defensive line on his team is. Stop running your year, month, day, without a game plan. Oprah doesn't just wake up and say let me see what today brings. No, her calendar is already planned out for months, sometimes, years in advance. Success just doesn't happen, it is planned in advance, and for me and many other successful people success is in our daily routine. Even the Bible says, "give us this day, our daily bread" because even God or the Creator (Universe) intended for us to have success daily. I can promise you this, once you are more intentional with your day, you will be more intentional with your life! Be mindful of the success you want to achieve and never stop until you get it!

CHAPTER TEN

On the Other Side of Pain

"Don't just go through it; grow through it."

Joel Osteen

Have you ever owned a favorite pair of jeans? Everything about those jeans just seemed to do you just right – the color, the style, and most importantly, the fit! Every time you did another load of laundry, you went looking for those jeans.

One day, you went to put on your favorite garment, and it seemed like they just didn't fit like they used to. You had to do a little bit more wiggling and a lot more jiggling to get into them. Two washes later, you just couldn't get into them at all. Even though you knew that you had outgrown them, you kept them in your drawer *just in case*. You figured that at some point, you might lose some weight and be able to fit into them once again.

Every morning when you go back into your dresser to find clothes to wear for the day, you would glance down and see those same jeans. Sadly, you would pass over them and wear something else, realizing three things:

- You are keeping something that is clearly of no further use to you. It has served its purpose in its own season, but yet you are still holding on to it wanting more.
- You are constantly feeling disappointed and feeling hurt when you see it, because you know that you really can't use it anymore. You are only holding on to memories.
- The comfort and emotional happiness that those jeans used to provide has now changed into something else. Now, it only serves to remind you that you are no longer the same person who used to value those jeans.

Buttercup used to have a peculiar saying, "Go ahead; keep on thinking that fat meat ain't greasy." It wasn't until I got much older that I realized what she meant by that. You can keep doing something or thinking something – living in your own personal fantasyland – if you want to. In reality, you know that you are expecting an outcome that you know you aren't going to get. That fat meat is going to stay greasy, no matter how much you want it not to be.

I know what it's like to be in a relationship that once made me smile and feel good. And I know what it feels like to be in love and feel appreciated by your partner. That was how it was between Boo and I in our best times. There wasn't anything that I wouldn't do for him, and I just knew there was nothing that he wouldn't do for me. We loved spending time together, and we couldn't stand to be apart. Being married seemed like a dream that had finally come true for me. Having his children was the icing on the cake.

Then, Boo began to stay out a little later at night. He wasn't home as much as he once was. What people don't seem to understand is that a relationship doesn't change overnight. If it did, then any sensible person would see the train wreck coming and end it right away. No, those jeans didn't get tighter overnight, either. Gradually, a millimeter at a time, they began to stretch a little more and a little more, until they finally wouldn't stretch anymore.

Sooner or later, that relationship that once had the perfect style, color, and fit starts to look and feel different. Happiness and contentment slowly turns into disappointment and eventually into depression and loneliness. You have to wiggle and jiggle a little bit more in order to make it fit. Two or three upsetting situations later, you come to the shocking realization that this relationship just doesn't fit anymore. Instead of coming to a mature and mutual agreement to end it, go our separate ways, and finally cut our ties, we throw it in that dresser drawer. We keep it, and hope that one day, maybe it will fit once again. Maybe if we both change our habits, it will work.

What really ends up happening is that now we are stuck with a relationship that we can't do anything with. We go to reach for those old comfy jeans, and we have to pull back our hand because we realize that they no longer serve the purpose that we are hoping for. Now, I'm lying next to a person that only brings me heartbreak and headaches.

We would argue about everything. What begins as "opposites attract" turns into "opposites annoy". It seems like nothing either of us do is right for the other. You may even begin to wonder how you ended up together in the first place. You may begin to question your own judgement. How did you end up falling in love with someone like this? How could someone who claimed to love you and want you for the rest of your life treat you so dirty and not seem to care how badly it is hurting you? The most hurtful feeling is reaching out for a companion only to realize that it's merely their physical being that is there with you. Their heart, their soul, mentally, emotionally, spiritually, and even financially, that person has long since been gone.

Have you ever kept a car that doesn't run just to be able to say that you have a car, but you still need to ask for a ride? Have you ever owned a pen that wouldn't write or a phone that won't dial? We all tend to keep things – and people – in our lives that no longer serve a purpose and that we have now outgrown. That isn't to say that they *never* served a purpose. Of course, they did, or we wouldn't have found the value in them in the first place. We all have heard that saying, "Some things are for a reason, some things are for a season, and some things are for a lifetime."

Many of us spend far too much time trying to make a Zebra change its stripes. A cheater is going to cheat. An addict is going to use. A liar is going to lie. An abuser is going to abuse. No matter how much of your life, your sex, your time, or your money you give to them, they are going to continue to do what they do, but now they get to do it with whatever resources you gave them as well. Unless they have truly changed their life and dedicated it to God mostly everything else is temporary, and that's real talk. Sometimes, it's not that they don't want to love you. Sometimes, it's that they truly don't know *how* to love you correctly. But here's the kicker – *and I want you to truly receive this* – it's NOT your job to teach them.

When someone starts to show us who they really are, we often filter out everything bad and try to keep the good. Once we have fallen in love, we want to believe in all of the good attributes. We want to think that they will change or grow out of the negative traits that they may have. It is natural to want to see the good in someone that you care about. Dr. Maya Angelou said, "When someone shows you who they are, believe them the first time." The truth of the matter is that we can't possibly change someone, no matter how good our intentions may be. No matter how badly you want to help them, they can only change themselves, and they must want to do so.

We are not only talking about romantic relationships here. You can't change your mother, your father, your teacher, your children, your business partner, boss, or your best friend, either! What you *can* do is decide for yourself whether you want to remain in a relationship with that person if it does not positively serve you. My grandmother used to say, "You can't get blood from a turnip." If someone is consistently showing you that you cannot rely on them for what you need, then why do you keep going back to the same dry well looking for water?

When you finally decide to end that relationship, you may go through a period of time where you feel horrible. You will probably cry and go through every bad emotion known to man. This is to be expected. You have been in that relationship for a very long time. You've grown accustomed to it. You can't imagine just letting go.

A natural reaction is to begin to start to feel down on yourself. Maybe it's *your* fault you begin to think. Why could I have done differently? You'll start seeking answers about why things have happened the way they have, and the easiest thing to do is to start pointing the finger. But, there will come a day when the emotion that you feel the most is relief and freedom. Things happened the way that they were supposed to. Life is not always fair, and every experience helps us to grow and learn. The amazing part about it is that now you are free to make new connections and memories with someone who *does* fit.

It is time to reevaluate some of the people, places, and things that are in your life right now. Are those things in season or out of season? Do they still serve a real purpose in your life, or are you holding onto old memories and emotions? It is true that you must learn to "let go and let God." When you close one door, another one will open for you – often much sooner than you think! I'll repeat it here again. You must trust the process. I found my purpose on the other side of my pain, and you will, too.

I was married for almost 15 years. I had told myself that I didn't believe in divorce. I just knew that I would never let that happen in my marriage. No matter how we tried to make things work, the season for our relationship was over. It became increasingly evident that we were headed down two different paths.

In the Bible, there is a verse that is often quoted many times.

> *"Be ye not unequally yoked together with unbelievers; for what fellowship hath righteousness with unrighteousness? And what communion hath light with darkness?"*

- 2 Corinthians 6:14

I would like to take the phrase "unequally yoked" a bit further. Do you know what a yoke is? It is a wooden beam with two big slots for the heads of two animals to slide into. These are usually used on oxen to enable the two animals to pull together on a load while working in pairs. This way, the two animals can use their combined strength to pull larger loads and get the job done faster and more efficiently.

If you yoke yourself to someone who is not your equal, it will do the opposite. You will make your life harder and less efficient. If one of you is headed one way and the other is headed somewhere else, now that you have put this yoke around the two of your necks, it is impossible for either of you to succeed. If one of you is far stronger than the other, how will you equally pull your load together without one person being overly tired and the other person just giving up completely?

Do you think that I wanted to become a single mother of three young children? NO! But the constant stress, strain, and frustration were literally killing me. I had been hospitalized. I had been suicidal several times during my marriage. I can remember cutting off everyone and everything, choosing to hibernate in my home for months on end.

#DisableYourLabels

The whole world knew that this man was cheating on me. He had even put up pictures and videos of himself with other females on social media. When I look back now, I think to myself, *Wow… what was I thinking?!*

Now I know that we should've ended the marriage years before we finally did. Maybe even before we added kids, cars, and houses to the equation, because all of those added connections simply added more stress to an already rocky situation. I'd never change a thing about having my children. They are a blessing to me every day, but the fact remains that it made it all the more difficult to end that relationship. Like most women, I had to consider long and hard how the breakup would affect my children. If you are a child or a product of a single parent home or have been affected by a divorce, I want you to know it's not your fault! You didn't do anything wrong, and both parents still love you even if one goes absent. They just may not know how to deal with the pain of the separation. There is no blueprint to parenting – it's kind of a trial by error type of thing. Because if we try to stay in a toxic situation, it will cause more harm and damage then anything else.

I'm not here to bash him; it's not as if we didn't have great times and make amazing memories along the way. The point is that you must recognize what season you are in, and you must move accordingly once you realize it. You are only postponing your own blessings by staying in a stagnant, unproductive situation. If there is too much dead weight on board, a ship will not float. The whole vessel will only sink.

DISABLE YOUR LABELS

There is a huge misconception about the word, "pain". People look at pain as something to stop or hinder them. I look at pain as a sign from God saying you're headed in the right direction. I look at pain as a growth tool now. Let me explain:

If you have ever worked out before or if you decided to work out after a long time, the next day your body is so sore that you can barely move or when you do move, you are in so much pain till you can't stand to move... lol. That pain isn't there to stop you from ever working out again, the pain reflects the growth of your muscles. Ever heard the term, "No pain, no gain"? A lot of times, pain will indicate an area you have grown or stretched in till the point it's no longer comfortable to move. Another way to look at pain is stepping out of your comfort zone, stepping outside of the norm and what you are used to. And when that thing that once brought pain to you becomes normal, or that area grows or stretches, it no longer bothers you. On the other side of the rain is the rainbow; everybody wants the beautiful rainbow, but without the rain. You can't have the testimony without the test. Everyone would love to have the breakthrough without the possibilities of breaking. The situation you are facing can make you bitter or better, but it can't do both. Disable the labels you are giving to the word pain.

During my lifetime, I have had many trials and many triumphs. I've been neglected. I have been raped. I've been molested. I've been in car accidents. I have been shot at, and almost died twice, all before the age of sixteen, and been locked up. I have been told that I would never have any children of my own. I've been abandoned and left for dead. I have been homeless. Nevertheless, I WON'T COMPLAIN! God has been so good to me. When I tell you that if He can bring you to it, He can bring you through it - I say it from experience.

Nobody could have convinced me years ago that the young Black girl from East 105th Street in Cleveland, Ohio would travel worldwide empowering others with her story. Nobody would have been able to tell me that I would have an anointing, that would inspire and impacting people's lives. How would I have ever known that I would one day be an international speaker, published author with friends, fans, and mentors all around the world? Could I have ever dreamed that I would host my shows encouraging others? That a once hopeless sixteen year old would grow to become the #1 sales agent in a celebrity charity event that would raise over 3.1 million dollar for The Florida Children's Hospital.

Rubbing elbows with different celebrities, PGA Champions, American top ranked tennis players, Super Bowl MVP's, Hall of Famers, Baseball Legends, & many entertainers just to name a few.

I have been on the very top of my game, and I have hit rock bottom. What I have learned through all of my experiences is expressed in another Dr. Maya Angelou quote: "When you get, GIVE. When you learn, TEACH." Also, from Galatians 6:7 in the Bible, "Be not deceived; God is not mocked: for whatever a man sow, that shall he also reap."

No matter what you are going through, please know that you are not alone, and it is just for a season. Pain and suffering do not last always. Your situation will not last forever. The American author and televangelist, Robert Schuller, wrote a book entitled, Tough Times Never Last, but Tough People Do! Remember that. If you remain hungry, striving for success, and working hard, you will persevere. Anything worth having is worth fighting for.

Never be ashamed of your struggle. No matter how awful your own story may seem, please know that there is nothing new under the sun. If you are going through it, someone else has gone, or will be going, through it, too! For many of us, dysfunction was our normal, but it is my hope and prayer that this book will somehow help you to find a new normal. I pray that you are able to find a new YOU and

#DisableYourLabels

"Disable Your Labels" No matter who is trying to label you a failure, doubt, stupid, inadequate, poor, fat, skinny, tall, short, nerd, dark skinned, light skinned, white trash, nigga, homo, butch, fag these are some of the words I hear hundreds of kids tell me they are being called, which means this is what you are being labeled! My dear King or Queen, My sweet Prince or Princess. You are worth so much more than what people, society, and our government has titled you as. YOU WALK WITH YOUR HEAD HELD HIGH AND FROM THIS DAY FORTH, YOU DISABLE THE LABELS OTHERS HAVE PLACED ON YOU!!! It's time for you to repackage your own label and YOU determine what that label will say in Jesus Name. I speak love, I speak life, and I speak liberty over your life today! I want you to go forth and walk in your greatness and understand your best days are ahead of you, and not behind you. I love you and wish you the best. Remember: "The only limits that exist are the ones that YOU create." Stay Encouraged.

WE ARE THE CHAMPIONS

(BONUS SECTION)

● ● ●

Stories of Overcoming Adversity

I am very pleased to be able to include the following section in this book. I have met some incredibly strong and resilient people in my life, and I've asked few of them to share their own experiences with you. In these next few pages, you will read their own truths, in their own words and completely unedited by me. Although vastly different, we all have gone through some form of dysfunction, and reading about each of our unique experiences can help to bridge the gap between us all.

I want to personally thank Naiomi, Ralph, Lisa, Kayla and Jayden for having the courage to share their hearts with the world. It's not easy allowing others to be inspired by your story of strength, but sometimes, the desire to help make it easier for someone else outweighs your fear of being judged or criticized. That is the magic, here. That is how lives are changed.

The Loudest Silence

by Naiomi Pitre

The pain in my ribs was immediate. The pain in my heart, on the other hand, had been gradually growing over the past four years. When my son's father rammed the large trash bin unto my body, that pain exploded like a detonated grenade. A massive sob unlike any other I had ever released came out of my mouth and sliced through the air around the staircase we stood on.

Just minutes before, he had slammed my business laptop shut and broke it. The same laptop that had all of my small business clients' work on it was now in pieces on our dining room table. That was the business that was making ends meet while he smoked up the money that he earned as a server. Cash tips are too easy to spend on the street before you decide to finally make it home.

After destroying my means of income, he grabbed the wooden doggy gate from the bottom of the stairs and smashed it into pieces, flying into a full-on rage. My son started screaming at the top of his lungs. The noise and clatter were enough to make anyone nervous, let alone an eighteen-month-old toddler. To make matters worse, the next victim of his anger was my son's favorite ride-on train toy. He picked it up and slammed it against the wall, shattering it into pieces and leaving a huge hole in the spot where it connected with the drywall. My son lost his mind.

As I held my son back from the hallway where his father was throwing his tantrum, the man who I will refer to as Danger stomped up the stairs and continued his tirade in my teenage daughter's room. Thankfully, she was not home, but he smashed her full-length mirror, leaving shards of glass on the carpet. Through my own tears, I held my baby boy to my chest and tried my best to comfort him.

I started thinking of a means of escape. I heard Danger coming back down. I backed away into the living room.

He stormed down the stairs and into the garage, dragging our large trash bin into the house and up the stairs.

"What are you doing?!" He asked, wide eyed.

"Cleaning up the glass!" He barked, impossibly dragging this big trash can up my staircase. The loud thumping as it hit each stair made my son jump in my arms. He was still shrieking, adding to the chaotic cacophony.

I placed my son in his playpen where he would be safe, and started up the stairs behind Danger. I foolishly tried to reason with him. I didn't want to just allow him to tear apart everything that we had built together, but I was about three years too late for that. Instead of listening to me, he rewarded my efforts by catching me in between the wall and the trash bin. He forcefully pushed the dumpster into my body over and over again, causing damage to my ribs, my wrists, and my knees as I tried to push it away from me. In the meantime, more holes were dug into the walls there, too, as I struggled to keep my balance.

The last blow he rendered after reaching around and striking me on my head several times with his fists, left me breathless. I couldn't catch a good breath of air for the life of me, and I stumbled down the stairs. Still trying to breathe, I picked up my son who was in full panic mode, and weakly carried him to the living room couch.

Gasping desperately for air, I watched my son cry so hard that he passed out against my chest. I looked down and made sure that he was still breathing, shaking him a little. He stirred a bit and frowned up his face but stayed unconscious. Not caring what happened at this point, all I cared about was getting him to a safe place.

I ran to the kitchen with my son in my arms and snatched the car keys from the counter. Completely barefoot, I dashed into the garage and hurriedly secured him into his car seat. I blocked out all of the shouting and noise that Danger was creating in the house, jumped into the front seat and pushed the remote to open the garage door. As I gunned the engine, I heard the door to the garage from the house slam open. I refused to look back and took off down our driveway.

That refusal to look back has been what I have held on to in the years following that awful day. I was able to find refuge in my mother's home, and completely dedicated myself to a plan of treatment involving intense therapy, counseling, church, and the kindness of family and friends. For so long, I had stayed quiet about many things that had been happening in our relationship. I finally stopped denying all of the dysfunction that had been occurring. Years and years of being silent, keeping horrible secrets, and trying to pretend that we were the perfect couple disintegrated that day.

I finally came clean to those who cared about me, and that allowed me to find my new normal. My prayer is that my story will give hope to someone else who is going through the hell of living a double life. Keeping secrets and pretending to be someone that you are not is a trap. It is a quick way to guarantee that you stay exactly where you are, because how can anyone help you escape if they don't even know that you are in trouble?

Diamond in the Rough

by Ralph Lopez

Growing up as a Mexican in L.A. was worse than you could imagine; it was rough. Not only did you have to survive living in my neighborhood, but you basically had one of two choices: 1) become a gang banger, or 2) become a drug dealer. The sad part is that they both had short-lived careers. It was 11 of us in a 4-bedroom house. My grandpa was doing everything he could to keep the family together, alive, and out of trouble, but there was only so much he could do. He would say to me every day, "Ralphie get an education, Ralphie get an education; son, if you want to make it out, stay educated." I said, "ok, ok Grandpa I got you." Not too long after that, I was expelled out of middle school and in Juvey. I felt like I let him down, but I promised that wouldn't happen again. But how? How do you make it out when no one else has done it before you? How do you make something of yourself when all you can see is drugs, murder, gang banging, and jobs wanting to pay you $3 an hour? It was then that I realized I had to blaze the trail for those siblings coming behind me; I had to show them something different. I could feel I was meant to do something different, and told myself I was going to find a way to make it somehow.

I watched my mother struggle. It seemed like all she could find was bulls**it job after bulls**it job, then she said, "something has to change." I believe the straw that broke the camel's back was when my 14-year-old sister got pregnant and her baby daddy was murdered, shot nine times before the baby was even born! My mother had had enough, so we moved out of L.A. when I turned 19, we moved to Las Vegas.

I hated Vegas at first as the people were rude; I missed my friends, family, and culture from L.A. but Vegas gave me a way out! School! I could hear my Grandpa's voice in the back of my head saying, "education is your way-out Ralphie." I was excited when I got accepted to C.S.N. as my dream of being a mechanic would finally come true. But now, we're back in the same boat of the lack of money. Sure, I was going to school to change my life and in the future, it would pay off, but what about the bills that were due now!? I needed a job; I needed income right now! I refused to fall into the sell drugs, rob, and gangbang mentality. My mom had a job at a call center around this time and she said she could get me on up there. I said, "cool". I didn't care if it paid $5 an hour, I just needed money now! I finally got the job; I was hungry, I started off at the bottom too, I mean $10 an hour (as if anybody could live off that), but I was grateful and made the best of every opportunity I had. Every call I would give it my all; I was focused, coming early, staying late, but still the first year I only made $8,000 humbly. That didn't stop me because I looked at it as the $8,000 my family didn't have. The next year was explosive! I made $60,000 that year, not bad for a 20-year-old with no experience. Now my eyes were wide open; if I could make $60,000, then I could make $100,000. I then got promoted to a commission-based only position & I BROKE RECORDS! Still, until this day I am the first 21-year-old to make $110,000 in a year, and I'm on track to do about $120,000 this year! I'm only 22 years old.

I send money to my Grandpa weekly and my mother is straight as well. Many times, we don't take advantage of every opportunity given to us. Imagine if I was unwilling to humbly accept that $10 an hour position, I would have missed the opportunity to make six figures a year. Trust and believe if I can do it, then you can do it. What I want you to take from my story is this:

1) *Focus on one thing at a time-* My number one focus was getting out of high school to graduate even with my setback of being expelled in middle school; it only meant that I just had to work harder.

2) *Take Advantage of EVERY OPPORTUNITY-* I would have never known I could make six figures if I would have quit, gave up or said I'm not taking a $10 an hour job. Even a diamond must go through heavy, heavy

amounts of pressure in order to form into a diamond. Disable Your Labels and remain humble.

YOUR STORY ALONE

BY LISA LANGLEY

E veryone has a story to tell, something they have faced, gone through; or even learned to deal with. But not everyone has to face their story alone. There is no such thing as normal. What is normal for me may not be normal for someone else. And because many kids and people get that confused, I want to share my story with you.

Growing up, I remember waking up in the middle of the night hearing an argument between my parents. I remember walking down the hallway, going left and then going into the living room where I could see my father and mom in front of the front door and my mom against the wall. They were shouting at each other. I just remember yelling at them to stop, and they told me to go to bed. The image has never left my mind. I was in 7th grade and remember this like it was yesterday.

My parents were very young when they had me. My mom was 15 and my dad was 19. By the time my mom was 22, she had 3 kids. I watched my parents struggle, and I watched their love for one another fade. They stayed together for us kids. My brothers were too young to understand, but I wasn't. Even though my parents tried to do what's best, both of them staying together only made it worse. Over the years I started to yell at my parents to get a divorce. I was tired of the fighting. I watched my dad become angry and my mom become depressed. When I was a sophomore in high school, they finally divorced. I lived with my mom in AZ and my brothers lived with my dad in CA. But the damage was already done.

My first relationship became a relationship of abuse. Many fights happened, I use to get hit in the head many times, I had multiple black eyes and I also went to jail twice, for domestic violence. I remember right after my birthday, I had a black eye from a fight and I went to my mom's house for dinner. I was so embarrassed about my black eye that I kept my sunglasses on in her house the entire time. I never took them off once hoping they would not see. That kind of relationship was all I knew. It was in the same relationship that I watched my parents be in growing up.

As this relationship came to an end, my life went down a very dark path. I made many bad choices that I cannot change. My biggest regret was being so caught up I was missed out on both my little brothers growing up. My life was going nowhere. I was headed on a path of ending up in prison or dead. I had to change it. And so, I made the decision to do just that.

I decided to join the Navy. I prepared for months, got clean, stopped making bad choices. With a court date in

December; I remember standing before the judge telling him I am ready to change my life and join the Navy and they released me. I went through all the processing and paperwork. Nothing could stand in my way... until my mom got the call. Everything changed.

Because of my second arrest, the Navy would not allow me to join. My heart broke and I was devastated. A relationship I had been trying so hard to get away from continued to follow me. I was angry and upset. I went to the Army recruiter the next day and talked to them and they said they could take me. I wanted to get out of AZ so fast that I just chose whatever job and went with it. This experience was something I will never forget. It was intense, scary and rewarding.

It's been 8 years since I made that choice. That decision. I disabled my labels and would not let my childhood control my present and future. I will not let the things I saw determine who I am. And I will be myself and make sure the choices I make are not my regrets. I am very successful where I am today. I went through quite the journey. Hit rock bottom a few times, but I got back up. I did not let anything dictate my life. I made the choice to change the things I did not like, and fix the things that were broken. It was not easy, but it was worth it. I live an amazing life now and a lot of things have changed. I no longer expect dysfunction in a relationship, in a friendship, or any type of partnership. I have an amazing career with a dream team that

I lead and we are like a family. I even drive my dream car brand new off the showroom floor. The new choices I made, made me who I am today. It's your story and your story alone, so make the choice to change it and rewrite it. You have to be the one to "Disable Your Labels" because only you can.

YOU DECIDE

BY KAYLA CZAPLA

J ust when I thought my relationship was completely over - a brand new chapter had just begun. Who wants to be alone? I mean really, it's scary, lonely, dull, especially when you had plans to spend the rest of your life with someone special. Then, reality hits you, they are no longer in your life, constant tears daily, the listening to sad songs, allowing yourself to be put in a mood of depression became common happenings. Constantly wondering their thoughts, actions, who they are with now, almost becomes an obsession. The what if's, was it me, and the famous am I good enough questions fills your head and heart daily.

Yeah, I know firsthand, I was there too. The person that once brought butterflies to my stomach, could put a smile on my face no matter what, and always had the right things to say, is now the main person bringing pain into my life. You get so locked up in your mind, what could have, should have, would have been, that it starts to take over and completely destroys you like a tornado. You feel nothing is going to get better even when people tell you it will; that's never helped me and it may not help you either. You start to give up because things seem so dull without them around; you've never known anything besides them. People used to tell me that I should go here, experience this, or try that to get my mind somewhere else, but it didn't last, most of the time it didn't even help. I've read tons of articles on how to get over someone and it always ends up with, "you'll move on", but you don't buy into it, you just can't. You won't because you feel you still have some sort of fire burning. I was trapped, for a total of 2 years after the relationship officially ended, but I trapped myself. So, what helped? Was there a medicine? A certain secret? No, there wasn't, I moved on when I was ready!

No one can tell you when to move on or how to move on. It's when YOU decide, but I will tell you this; when you do decide, it's like finding the pot of gold at the end of the rainbow. Felt like you were never going to get to it, but you did. I can officially say I've closed that door and put a deadbolt lock on it and will never unlock it again. I've seen the damage it can cause to your friends, family, career, and you. Once you've closed the door, good things start happening and you ask why this didn't happen a long time ago! It's because you were still holding on to the anchor that kept dragging you down. I can also say I got an amazing promotion at my job that people wait a lifetime to receive literally. I am responsible for several departments that I help to run worldwide, I am the Vice President and I'm only 23 years old. Which goes to show hard work really does pay off. I enjoy life again; my smile is brighter than ever and more importantly, I love me again! I couldn't have done any of this if I didn't help myself escape. I did it though, I really did it, and for you, it may seem like it will never get better, but it will, once YOU DECIDE.

DISABLE YOUR LABELS

There is a scripture in Deuteronomy 28:6 that says, "Blessed shalt thou be when thou comest in, and blessed shalt thou be when thou goest out."

The problem is this, people understand they are good, great, excited, happy to go into the situation. It can be a relationship, a job, a new school, or new environment, but why when it's time to end that thing you feel like it's the end of the world? Some people really feel suicidal after they lose a scholarship, relationship, job, partnership, internship at their dream location, etc. Not realizing that they were even more blessed to come out of the situation then before they went into it. NEVER get so caught up in a person, place, or thing that you feel or believe it defines you. My grandmother used to say, "They aint make you, and they can't break you."

LAST MAN STANDING

BY JADEN

They didn't even let Jayden go to the funeral. The Juvenile Detention Facility said "they don't transport inmates to funerals if the death was violence-related." But, what they didn't understand was that this was more than a brother to Jayden, this was like a father and his last living brother. Jayden was the youngest of the three, Jason his oldest brother, and Mike, his middle brother just two years older than him. Jason, his eldest brother would have been 28 years old this year if he hadn't been murdered five years prior.

Jason was the eldest of the three. "Growing up on the Westside, our mother would borrow money from a friend till she got paid the following Friday, and this was a weekly survival skill." But, Jason was tired of living that life of begging, borrowing, or barely making it to the next day. So at the age of 15, he became a robber, stick up kid, home invader. He would go to the good neighborhoods and do a B & E (breaking and entering) The more he stole, the more he wanted to steal. It was like a treasure hunt he never knew what he was going to find. And everything was business as usual. As they began to pick the lock, turn the door to open the door to this house, the alarm was triggered and an unfamiliar voice yelled, "Kathy is that you?" And in that moment, everything said leave! Turn around! Someone was home! But this was an old man and all they had to do was wave the gun in his direction and he would lay down. From what the streets said, Jason and his 2 goons made their way up each stair, slowly, and quietly as possible to catch the old man off guard. They received a rude awakening as he was standing there with a fully loaded shot gun. Jason was the first to make it to the top of the stairs, when the old man was already cocked and loaded. Once he pulled the trigger, the gun let off what seemed like an explosion in Jason's chest and his body flew past his other 2 friends that were following behind him, as his body landed at the bottom of the stairs. "My brother laid there with a hole in his chest that you could see right through." As his friends ran and watched in horror. "They didn't even wait for the body to hit the ground completely before they ran out and left him right there." Jayden remembers

"I was just a kid at that time, almost thirteen to be exact." Says Jayden, but I remembered all the gifts, clothes, fun times we had, he was my protector, my provider. I didn't care if he was robbing, all I cared about was that he was my brother, and the new Marvels movie was coming out on Saturday and the new Jordans, and we had plans to go to the mall, then to the movies after that." But instead, Jayden would sadly be attending the funeral that Saturday of his own hero the only father figure he had ever known. That day will never be the same for Jayden and Mike the only two brothers left. Sadly, Mike would pick up where Jason left off.

Everyone deals with death differently. Mike began to smoke weed and drank as a way to cope with his brother's death. It was just a little weed, no big deal. But weed was just a gateway drug and it was just a matter of time before the smoke and drink wasn't enough, and Mike began to pop prescription pills. Mike eventually got caught up in the street life, got hooked on pills & drugs, dating multiple women, crime, fighting, and banging. Not even two years after his Jason's death, Mike got arrested for battery and was sentenced to 18 months in the Juvenile Detention Center. He was only 16 years old at the time, they said he was out of control, a hot head with a temper out of this world. So now, Jason is dead, and Mike is in jail, and Jayden was stuck trying to figure out how to deal with all these drastic changes that just happened in his life in the last 2 and a half years.

Fourteen years old and now Jayden was the man of the house. His mother was really struggling to keep money on Mike's books, feed them, pay the rent, all while the light was getting cut off. He now understood all the pressure his brothers were under. Then he tried to go through Jason's route, and rob a 7/11 store but got caught, and the Judge let him off with a warning of 2 years on probation. A year had passed and Mike was coming home, Jayden couldn't be more excited. Soon as Mike hit the streets he ran wanted to get high and kick it with the homies, and Jayden was right under him watching his every move. The homies got in a fight and Jayden was right there fighting or not, it landed him in the #1 place he didn't want to be when the police came. In jail!! This was a probation violation.

"I can still remember the exact spot I was laying on my bunk" when the officer called out "Johnson, you got a visitor." Jaden says, "A visitor?" It wasn't his visiting time nor his visiting day. "This can't be right I thought." As he made his way to the officer as they escorted him to what looked like a private office, Jayden was so confused. "I know that they were not trying to interrogate me, or get me to snitch. Are they?" "It wasn't until I saw the white collar on the Chaplin that I knew this was no average visit." "It's like I could feel my heart beat through my chest, it was pounding faster and faster, louder and louder, all the thoughts began to overtake me. When they take you to the Chaplin, that means death!" "Now, who? Was it my mother? No, I just spoke with her. Was it my grandmother? She was old and feisty. I began to think that she was immortal: no pneumonia, no cancer, or no infection could kill her. Or was it my absent father that I had never seen only heard stories of, and claims that I was his splitting image? But, the worst was yet to come, it seemed as if the air escaped my lungs, and body went into shock when they said they found my brother, Mike, dead at the scene of a crime. It was a shot out at a party and they said he died on the spot. I couldn't produce a word that could explain the pain that I felt when I heard those words. My heart hadn't even begun to heal from Jason's death, and not even 3 years later, you are telling me Mike is gone too?" That was the beginning of a downward spiral for Jayden. He didn't care about people, he didn't care about life! And to top it all off, The Juvenile Detention Facility won't let Jayden attend Mike's funeral.

DISABLE YOUR LABELS

We all make choices in life but we never think about how those choices effect those we love. Jayden was a victim of the pain, environment, bad choices and examples set forth by those he loved and admired. Have you ever took into account the indescribable pain, frustration, fears, and abandonment we bring on others that we love when we make irresponsible decisions? Do you think Jason thought he was giving Mike and Jayden a blueprint to death and destruction? Have you thought about the path you are creating for those that come after you? Rather it's a brother, sister, niece, nephew, baby cousin or even a best friend. Anyone can lead someone down a wrong road, but it takes true leadership, heart, drive, hope, love, and vision to lead someone down the right path in life especially when NO ONE before you has done it. I once heard a flight attendant say "As a courtesy can you please leave the plane cleaner than you found it for the next passengers that come after you?" What if we looked at our families this way, our communities, our schools, our relationships with others? What if we left our families better than we found it, what if we leave our schools better than we found it. What if we leave a relationship with someone better than we found them, instead of them being broken, battered and bitter once our relationship is over?

Disable the Labels on thinking someone is going to change your family, raise the bar for your situation, or believe in your abilities. I have a saying "If its meant to be, it's up to me!" Don't wait for someone else in your family to raise the bar, or make the 1st million if it's meant to be it's up to YOU! I love you, I believe in you and let it be said I lived everyday of my life to help, empower, impact, inspire and transform you into the beautiful men and women of God that you are called to be. Let it be said that when it's all said and done " Desirae King left this generation, this earth, this world, city, state, this community, this family a better than when she found it!" And I am speaking the same over YOU TODAY!

ABOUT THE AUTHOR

Motivational Speaker and Life Coach, Desirae King

Desirae King is an award-winning international speaker, evangelist, lifestyle strategist, and Certified Life Coach. She is an in-demand keynote speaker for corporate settings, conferences, schools, churches, empowerment seminars, and more. Her first book, *Disable Your Labels*, encourages readers to break away from the label's others have put on them, and to shape themselves into the person they've always imagined themselves to be.

Ms. King has more than two decades of sales experience. She has received over 25 #1 sales and high-performance achievements awards, for several Fortune 500 companies, including Avis Car Rental, Dollar Thrifty Car Rental, and Diamond Resorts. On top of that her commission-based sales exceeding $6,000,000 in additional company revenue. Desirae's singular skill has landed her guest appearances on multiple nationally syndicated radio shows, and a feature in *The Recorder*, one of the largest faith-based magazines in the country.

Desirae non-profit initiatives allowed her to be the top

earner for a nationally syndicated televised celebrity charity event, that raised more than $3,000,000 for the Florida Hospital for Children (now AdventHealth for Children). As well as collaborations with PGA Tour champions, Super Bowl MVPs, top-ranked tennis players, baseball legends, and numerous celebrities.

Far from the rough and tough life she once lived. Ms. King is the living example that once you "Disable Your Labels" you can live a life you deserve. The need for others to hear her impactful message of survival, transformation, and self-empowerment inspired Desirae to create the Transpireful Network. Through this company, she can connect with people who have a desire for a clearer vision and a more defined purpose and propel them towards success, despite what their background and upbringing may be.

A busy mother of 3, Desirae still finds time to speak at myriad events and host the "Morning Manna" Bible-based leadership call where, as in all her work, she teaches followers to disable their labels and **take back their power**. Feel free to Join in Monday – Friday

www.Bit.ly/praydaily05 or FB Live @DesiraeInspires

#DisableYourLabels

For more information on the author, you can check out her website:
www.DisableYourLabels.com

OR follow her on social media to get inspired and motivated:
@DesiraeInspires on Instagram, Snapchat, Twitter, Facebook, and YouTube
OR search #DesiraeInspires #DisableYourLabels

Made in the USA
Lexington, KY
25 October 2019